How to Train Your
Labrador Retriever

liz palika

LABRADOR RETRIEVER

Photos by the author unless
otherwise credited.

The publisher would like to thank Elizabeth Tomao and her Labrador Retriever Lucy for contributing photos to this book.

Distributed in the UNITED STATES to the Pet Trade by T.F.H. Publications, Inc., One T.F.H. Plaza, Neptune City, NJ 07753; on the Internet at www.tfh.com; in CANADA Rolf C. Hagen Inc., 3225 Sartelon St. Laurent-Montreal Quebec H4R 1E8; Pet Trade by H & L Pet Supplies Inc., 27 Kingston Crescent, Kitchener, Ontario N2B 2T6; in ENGLAND by T.F.H. Publications, PO Box 15, Waterlooville PO7 6BQ; in AUSTRALIA AND THE SOUTH PACIFIC by T.F.H. (Australia), Pty. Ltd., Box 149, Brookvale 2100 N.S.W., Australia; in NEW ZEALAND by Brooklands Aquarium Ltd. 5 McGiven Drive, New Ply-mouth, RD1 New Zealand; in SOUTH AFRICA, Rolf C. Hagen S.A. (PTY.) LTD. P.O. Box 201199, Durban North 4016, South Africa; in Japan by T.F.H. Publi-cations, Japan—Jiro Tsuda, 10-12-3 Ohjidai, Sakura, Chiba 285, Japan. Pub-lished by T.F.H. Publications, Inc.
MANUFACTURED IN THE UNITED STATES OF AMERICA
BY T.F.H. PUBLICATIONS, INC.

Contents

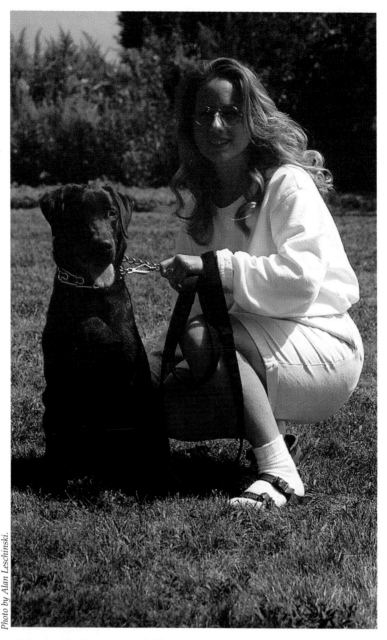

Labrador Retrievers are probably the most popular dog in America. They achieved this status because they are extremely friendly, intelligent and VERY trainable.

labrador retriever

INTRODUCTION

I have been teaching dog obedience classes for over 20 years and see, on the average, just over a thousand dogs and owners per year. Through the years, I have seen a number of different breeds rise and fall in popularity. For a few years, German Shepherd Dogs were the rage, Poodles came and went,

Prospective owners also need to know that there are other options than simply buying a puppy. Puppies are a lot of work and take a long time to grow up. Adopting an older puppy, a young adult, or even a mature dog might be a better choice for many people.

In this book, I have tried to

Photo by Isabelle Francais.

Labrador Retrievers were originally used in Labrador to retrieve birds that were shot down.

then Cocker Spaniels. Today, Labrador Retrievers are the breed of choice for many people.

As an obedience instructor, I always have misgivings when people buy the "popular" breed and Labs are no exception. Now, don't get me wrong, Labs are nice dogs! However, they are not the right dog for everyone. Prospective dog owners need to understand the breed they are considering—whether it is a Lab, a Golden, a Cocker, or any other breed.

present Lab owners (and prospective Lab owners) with choices about choosing a dog and good effective information as to how to make that dog a well-behaved member of the family. Labs can be fun-loving, energetic clowns as well as serious, hard-working dogs. With training and help from their owner, they can be a friend, a partner, and a great companion.

SELECTING
the Right Dog for You

WHAT ARE LABRADOR RETRIEVERS?

Labrador Retrievers (Labs) are thought to have originated in Labrador, Canada, and were originally bred to retrieve birds for hunters. Hard-working, versatile dogs able to retrieve in the roughest of conditions, the breed became a favorite for both sport hunters and for field trial and gun dog trial competitors.

Today, however, Labs have become a popular pet dog. Mary Feazell, a Labrador Retriever expert and breeder, said that pet Labs are, "Perpetual Ego Transformers who lick tears, lower blood pressure, dance at laughter, and always, always love you." ("Pets and Great Pets" by Mary Feazell, *The Official Book of the Labrador Retriever,* Dr. Bernard W. Ziessow, Editor, TFH Publications, 1995.)

Labrador Retrievers are fun-loving, playful, friendly dogs and very much in love with people.

labrador retriever

Temperament

Labrador Retrievers are fun-loving, energetic dogs. Very people oriented, Labs need to spend time with their owners; time to play, exercise, learn obedience skills and social rules and even just have quiet time. This desire to be with people affects all aspects of his life. A Lab is not a good dog to be left alone in the backyard all day. When bored and lonely, the Lab may become destructive, digging up the yard, ripping up your garden, or tearing up the garden furniture. In a desire to be with people, some Labs become incredible escape artists; jumping fences or digging out of the yard. Because of this people orientation, Labs make poor watchdogs. Although many Labs will bark when people approach the yard or house, most Labs will, instead, lick the burglar's face!

Labrador Retrievers are the dog of choice for many guide dog schools because they are so trainable.

However, this love for people has positive aspects, too. Labs can be incredible working dogs, sometimes serious to a fault. Labrador Retrievers are the breed of choice for many guide and service dog schools and in many schools have replaced the German Shepherd Dog, a breed that held the position of supreme working dog for many years. Labs today are serving quite capably as guide dogs, service and assistance dogs, therapy dogs, drug detection dogs, bomb detection dogs, arson detection dogs, and much, much more.

Don't let this ability to work fool you, though. Labs can and will find the fun in anything. Puppies will play with anything; chasing butterflies, balls, toys, and even airplanes high in the sky. Even grownup, mature adults retain a sense of fun and will turn into a clown when given any excuse to do so. If

If you think owning one Lab is fun, try two!

you decide to add a Labrador Retriever to your life, you had better like to laugh!

Physical Appearance

Labrador Retrievers are medium-sized dogs, usually between 21 and 25 inches tall and 55 to 80 pounds in weight. The bitches (females) are smaller, lighter in weight, and more feminine in appearance than the dogs (males). Labrador Retrievers are incredibly strong for their size with tremendous stamina. Labs have a medium short, coarse, waterproof coat and come in three colors: black, chocolate, and yellow. No other colors are acceptable. Labs should give the appearance of a well-balanced dog that is able to work and work hard.

IS A LAB THE RIGHT DOG FOR YOU?

Evaluating Your Personality and Lifestyle

The decision to add a dog to your family is not a decision that should be taken lightly. This is a 14 to 15 year commitment and although Labrador Retrievers are, for the most part, easy going dogs, they do have some specific needs.

Do you work long hours and come home tired, just wanting to relax, spending the evening reading or watching television? If you do, then a calm, older Lab might be good for you. Do you come home tired but like to get outside, walking or riding your bicycle? If so, a calm adult dog might suit your needs. Do you work at home, have short work hours and enjoy doing things? If so, a puppy or an active young dog should please you.

Being the center of a dog's world can be thrilling to some people and overwhelming to others. If you don't like being followed, watched, or touched, don't get a Labrador Retriever. A Lab will want to follow you from room to room and will be heartbroken even if you go to the bathroom without him. When you sit down, the Lab will want to lie on your feet or climb into your lap. When you leave the house, the Lab will want to go with you. Obviously, having a dog with you 24 hours a day is impossible for most people; however, if you own a Lab, you will need to be able to provide as much companionship as possible.

What is your life like? Are you retired and live alone? If your health is good, either a puppy or an adult Lab might be a good dog for you. Are there active children in the house? Labs can be wonderful with children as long as there is adult supervision and the dog is taught good social rules. However, if you work full time and live alone, a Lab might not be the best choice—as was mentioned earlier, a Lab alone is a lonely, unhappy dog.

given a chance, will wander off to explore. A large yard is wonderful, but even a dog run (no smaller than 10 feet by 30 feet) is acceptable as long as the dog gets plenty of time out of the run with you.

You must also have some means of exercising the dog. If you like to go jogging, that's

It is doubtful that there is a more affectionate breed than Labrador Retrievers.

The Dog's Needs

Before you decide to add a Labrador Retriever to your family, make sure you can fulfill the dog's needs. First of all, your time and companionship is of the utmost importance. As was mentioned earlier, Labs do very poorly alone in a backyard all day. This is a companion breed who needs to spend time with you.

You will also have to have a securely fenced yard. As a bird dog, Labs are very curious and

fine, but if you are not a jogger you will need to think of an alternative. Perhaps you can teach the dog to run next to your bicycle, or you can take the dog swimming on a regular basis. A young, healthy Lab is NOT a couch potato!

SELECTING THE RIGHT DOG

Male or Female?

There are a lot of myths concerning the personality

traits of both males and females. Ultimately it depends upon the personality of the individual dog.

Dogs that are neutered or spayed are usually a little calmer than intact Labs.

MONEY MATTERS

Do you have the financial means to care for this dog? Good quality food is not cheap, nor is veterinary care. Your dog will need vaccinations, regular check ups and will need to be spayed or neutered. You will need groom-ing supplies, including brushes, nail clippers, and flea and tick control products. Your dog will need a collar, a leash or two and a kennel crate. You will also need to invest in an obedience class (or two!). Also, at some point during the dog's lifetime, there may be an emergency veterinary call because of an injury or ill-ness. You will need the financial resources to care for your dog and must never delay needed care because of a lack of money.

Spayed and neutered bitches and dogs are usually a little calmer than those that are not because spaying and neutering removes the sexual hormones and as a result, the sexual tension that can accompany those hormones. To be a good pet and companion, your Lab doesn't need those hormones anyway.

What Age?

Puppies are adorable, especially Lab puppies. When you add a puppy to your family it is just like adding a baby to your family. In fact, in many ways, raising a puppy is much like raising a child except that the puppy will grow up faster. As the puppy learns and grows, it will become an integral part of your family and by the time your puppy has grown up (three years or so), your young Labrador Retriever will have become a good friend.

However, it takes a lot of work to raise a puppy and for many people, adding a puppy to their life might not be the best choice. But that doesn't mean those people cannot have a dog. There are many adult Labrador Retrievers needing homes and these dogs could be just the answer for people who do not have the time to spend with a young puppy. With an adult dog, you know what you're getting. You know how big the dog is, what the adult personality is like, and the state of the dog's health. With a puppy, some of these things are unknown until the puppy grows up.

RESCUE GROUPS

Many breed clubs also sponsor or run breed rescue groups. Rescue groups screen the dogs they take in for adoption. Dogs are checked for personality or temperament flaws (such as aggression) and their obedience skills (or lack thereof) are evaluated. The dogs are vaccinated, and if needed, spayed or neutered. This screening process can be invaluable to you, the potential adopter. To find a Lab rescue group in your area, call the Labrador Retriever Club of America rescue coordinator.

There are, of course, some negative factors about adopting an adult dog. Adopting an adult is sometimes like buying a used car; you don't know how it has been treated prior to your ownership and that can affect future behavior. Many times, too, the adult dog's past health history is unknown. Newly adopted adult dogs also must have time to settle into their new homes; time must be allowed for emotional and physical adjustment.

Finding an Adult Dog

If you have decided that an adult Lab would be better for you, there are many places to find the right dog. Many Labs are given up by their owners for a variety of reasons; some didn't research the breed and found after a few months that a Lab was not the right breed for them. Other people may not have been willing to give their Lab the time and training the dog needed. Or perhaps there was an emergency, the owner may have passed away and family members were unable to keep the dog. Check for these dogs at your local humane society or shelter.

Once in a while, guide dog and service dog schools will have dogs available for adoption. There might be a young dog who washed out of the training program or an older retired dog that can no longer work. These dogs are normally very well socialized and incredibly well trained.

Evaluating an Adult Dog

Once you have found an adult Labrador Retriever that

you like, how do you decide whether this is the right dog for you? Well, emotions certainly play a part—do you like this dog? There is more of a chance of success in this new

Sometimes you can adopt a well-trained Lab from a guide dog school.

relationship if you and the dog like each other. However, there should be more to the decision-making process than just emotions.

Do you know why the dog was given up by its first owners? Sometimes the dog is given up through no fault of its own—maybe its owner was transferred overseas or passed away. However, if the owner gave the dog up because of behavior problems, you need to know that. Has the dog had any obedience training? Is the dog housetrained? These are important issues; housetraining a previously untrained adult Lab can be a task!

What is the dog's personality like? When you whistle or speak to the dog, does he look at you happily, wagging his tail? If he does, great. If he looks sideways at you, slinks or bares his throat, be careful. He could be afraid, or worried because of previous mistreatment, but an unknown fearful dog might also bite. Be careful, too, if the dog stares at you, making eye contact, without wagging his tail. This could be a potentially aggressive dog.

Ideally, you want a dog that is happy to see you without showing too much worry or fear and without showing any aggression. You want a dog that is housetrained and who has had some obedience training. Make sure that the dog's behavior problems are ones that you can live with for the time being and are willing to work on in the future.

Ideally, too, the dog has already been spayed or neutered, is vaccinated and is healthy.

Finding a Puppy

If you have the time, the resources and patience to raise a puppy, you will want to find a reputable breeder. Breeder referrals can come from many

Your local pet shop sells excellent grooming supplies, which can sometimes be purchased in affordable combination packages. Photo courtesy of Wahl, USA.

sources. People walking their dog might refer you to their breeder. A veterinarian, groomer, or trainer may know of some reputable breeders. Many of the national dog magazines have classifieds where breeders can advertise. You might also want to attend a dog show in your community and talk to the people attending the show.

Once you find a few breeders, ask for an appointment to meet with them. At your meeting, ask the breeders a few questions. "Are you active in the dog world?" This answer will tell you many things. First, if the breeders show their dogs in conformation competition, their dogs are probably good examples of the breed. If they show in obedience competition, their dogs are trainable. If they show their dogs in field or gun dog trials, their dogs have the working instincts Labs are supposed to have.

"Do you belong to the Labrador Retriever Club of America as well as local or regional clubs?" If breeders do, they are more likely to be up to date on news about the breed. Breed club newsletters and magazines usually publish health related issues, including genetic or inherited problems and potential treatments.

You can have your choice of three colors!

"What health problems have you seen in your dogs?" If the breeders say none, be skeptical. A breed or line with no health problems is rare. Labrador Retrievers can have a number of health problems, including hip and elbow dysplasia, joint and bone disorders, epilepsy, cataracts and other eye disorders, allergies, and dwarfism. Reputable breeders should be honest with you about potential health problems and what they are doing to try and prevent future problems.

"Can you provide me with a list of references?" Keep in mind that this list will consist of people the breeder knows are happy with their dogs, but it can still serve a purpose. You can still ask them about their experience. "Did the breeder work well with them? Would they buy from the breeder again?"

Caring breeders will ask you as many questions as you ask them. They want to know if you are the right person to buy one of their puppies. Don't get defensive; they are trying to do the right thing. Instead, answer the questions honestly. If by some chance, a particular breeder says that her dogs are not right for you, listen to her, she knows her dogs better than you.

Evaluating a Puppy

Each puppy has his own personality and finding the right personality to match with yours is sometimes a challenge. For example, if you are outgoing, extroverted and active, a quiet, withdrawn, submissive puppy would not fit well into your household and lifestyle. You will need a puppy more like you. However, that quiet puppy might do very well for a quiet person or a less active retiree.

When you go to look at a puppy or a litter of puppies, there are a few things you can do with the puppy to help evaluate the puppy's personality. First, with the puppy away from his mother and littermates, place the puppy on the ground and walk a few steps away. Squat down and call the puppy to you. An outgoing, extroverted Lab puppy will come happily and

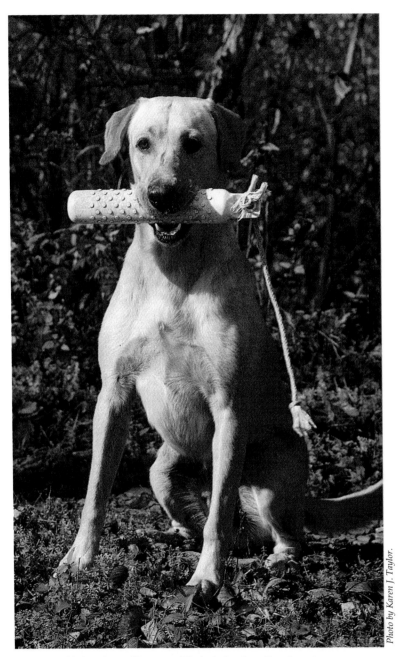

Photo by Karen J. Taylor.

Responsible breeders will screen all Labs before breeding them to ensure against genetic diseases and produce the best quality puppies.

try to climb into your lap. If you stand up and walk away, the extrovert will follow you, trying to get under foot. If you crumple up a piece of paper and throw it six feet away, he

Remember that Labs are active and love to play. If you are a retiree, an adult Lab may be better suited to your lifestyle.

will dash after it and bring it back proudly. This Lab would do well with an owner who is just as much an extrovert as he is. He will need training, lots of exercise and a job to occupy his mind.

A quiet submissive puppy will come to you when you call but may do a belly crawl, or may roll over and bare her belly. When you get up to walk away, the submissive puppy may watch you but may be hesitant to follow you. If you toss the piece of paper for her, she may go after it, may bring it part way back but may be hesitant to bring it directly to you. This puppy will need a

quiet owner, gentle handling, and positive training to build her confidence.

These two puppies are the extremes; most Labs are somewhere in between these two personality types. Try to find a puppy with a personality that will be comfortable with you, your personality, your family and your lifestyle. Don't get a pushy, dominant puppy and hope to change him; he may learn control with training but he will always have that personality. Nor should you get the quiet submissive puppy because you feel sorry for her. Find the puppy who is right for you.

BE CAREFUL!

Adding a dog to your family should be a time of anticipation and excitement, but it also requires thought, research and preparation to prevent the experience from becoming a nightmare. Unfortunately, horror stories abound of purebred dogs plagued with health problems, or breeders who misrepresented their dogs or who didn't come through with the promised paperwork. Hopefully, this Labrador Retriever will be a part of your life for the next 12 to 14 years, so make sure a Lab is the right dog for you and choose him carefully.

Canine
DEVELOPMENT
Stages

IN THE BEGINNING

Even though dogs and people have lived together for thousands of years, the bond that we have with dogs must be renewed with each puppy. The bond itself is not hereditary although the tendency and ability to bond are. Labrador Retrievers, as a breed, are known for their ability to bond closely with their owners. This relationship between a dog and owner is what makes owning a dog so special. To understand when and how the bond develops, it's important to understand that a dog is a unique creature, not a person in a fuzzy dog suit.

FAMILIES AND PACKS

Most researchers agree that thousands of years ago the first domesticated dogs were descended from wolves. Wolves are very social creatures and live in an extended family pack.

The pack might consist of a dominant male and a dominant female (usually the only ones who breed) as well as a few subordinate adults, juveniles and puppies. This is a very harmonious group who hunt together, play together, defend their territory against intruders and care for each other and the pack's young. The only discord happens when there is a change in the pack order. If an adult of some status dies or leaves the pack, or if a youngster tries to assume dominance, there might be some jockeying around to fill that position.

Many experts feel that domestic dogs adapt so well to our lifestyle because we also live in groups although our groups are called families instead of packs. However, the comparison really isn't accurate; our families are much more chaotic than the average wolf pack! We are terribly inconsistent with our social rules and rules for behavior. (We let the dog up on the couch when he's clean but yell at him when he jumps up with muddy paws!) To the dog our communication skills are confusing. Our voice says one thing while our body language says another. We tell "white lies" to spare someone's feelings; our dogs don't understand "white lies." To our dogs, people are very complex, confusing creatures. So yes, we can say that both dogs and humans live in social groups and we can use that comparison to understand a little more about our dogs; however, we must also understand that our families are very different from a wolf pack.

FROM BIRTH TO FOUR WEEKS OF AGE

For the first three weeks of life, the family and the pack are unimportant as far as the baby Labrador Retriever is concerned. The only one of any significance is his mother. She is the key to his survival and is the source of food, warmth, and security.

At four weeks of age, the baby Lab's needs are still centered on his mother but his littermates are becoming more important. Littermates provide warmth and security when mom leaves the nest. During this period he will learn to use his senses to follow sounds and to focus his eyes. His curiosity about the world around him is developing and he will start exploring his nest or whelping box.

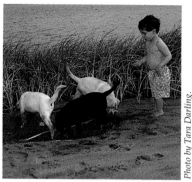

There just isn't anything more charming than a Lab puppy.

Mom will also start disciplining the puppies now and her instinctive training is vitally important to the puppies' future acceptance of discipline and training. We can also learn a lot by watching mom discipline her babies.

MOTHER LOVE

Shadow is a Black Labrador Retriever, an American Kennel Club conformation champion and an obedience Utility Dog. She is also a very good mother. When one of her puppies bites too hard, her correction is short, sharp, fair, and firm: a growl and a muzzle bite that ceases as soon as the puppy reacts submissively. Every correction is followed by love and affection and she never holds a grudge.

The breeder should be handling the puppies during this period, gentling touching and massaging them. The puppies will learn the difference between their mom's caresses and those from people.

WEEKS FIVE THROUGH SEVEN

The baby Lab goes through some tremendous changes between five and seven weeks of age. He is learning to recognize people and is starting to respond to individual voices. He is playing more with his littermates and the wrestling and scuffling teaches each puppy how to get along, how to play, when the play is too rough, when to be submissive, and what to take seriously. Mom's discipline at this point teaches the puppy to accept discipline, correction, training, and affection.

This is a good time for the puppy to meet other people. The breeder should supervise all visits so that the puppy isn't handled too roughly or frightened, of course, but friendly handling and play will help socialize the puppy with people.

If the puppy is taken from his mother and littermates during this time frame, he may have lasting behavioral problems. He may have difficulty dealing with other dogs, may have problems accepting rules and discipline and may turn excessively shy or excessively aggressive because of fear.

THE EIGHTH WEEK

The eighth week of life is a frightening time for most puppies. Puppies go through several periods of fear growing up and this is the first one. Even though this is the traditional time for most puppies to go to their new homes, they would actually benefit tremendously from staying with their mom and littermates for one more week. If the puppy leaves his breeder's home during the eighth week of life and is frightened by the car ride to his new home, he may retain that fear of car rides for the rest of his life. The same applies to his new home, new sounds in the

Most Lab pups are not ready to go to a new home until they are nine weeks of age or older.

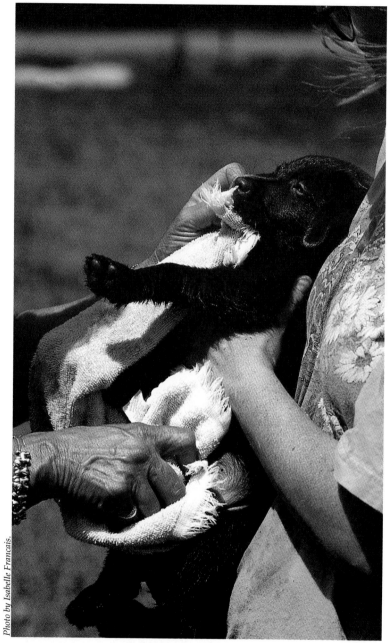

Photo by Isabelle Francais.

Tiny Lab puppies are great to cuddle, but soon become large adults. Early training will stop problems before they start.

house, the trip to the veterinarian's office, or anything else that frightens him.

WEEKS NINE TO TWELVE

The baby Lab can go to his new home anytime during the ninth and tenth weeks of life. At this age, he is ready to form permanent relationships. Take advantage of this and spend time with your new puppy, playing with him, cuddling with him and encouraging him to explore his new world. Teach him his name by calling him in a high pitched tone of voice, especially when he is already moving towards you. (Never use his name to scold him!) Encourage the puppy to follow you by backing away from him, patting your leg, or clapping your hands.

Socialization is very important now. Socialization is more than simply introducing your puppy to other people, dogs, noises and sounds. It is making sure that your baby Lab is not frightened by these things and that he is introduced to them gradually. For example, after your baby Lab has had some vaccinations (check with your veterinarian), take your puppy with you to the pet store when you go to buy some dog

food. While there, introduce your puppy to the clerks, other customers and even to the store parrot. Your trip there could also include walking up some stairs, walking on slippery floors and going through an automatic door. All of these things, introduced gradually and with a lot of encouragement, and repeated all over town, add up to a confident, well-socialized puppy.

During this time frame, pack instincts are developing and you can use this stage of growth to teach your puppy his position in the family. Each and every day, have each member of the family roll the puppy over and give him a tummy rub. This exercise may seem very simple but by baring his tummy, he is assuming a submissive position to family members. When his mom corrected him, he would roll over and bare his tummy to her; here, he's doing it for you.

When your baby Lab is 11 and 12 weeks old, discipline becomes more important. Love, attention and security are still vital, of course, but your puppy is now ready to learn some basic household rules. Don't allow him to do anything now, such as stealing food, jumping on people or bouncing off the furniture, that you are not going to want him to do later, when he's full grown.

RETRIEVING

Begin retrieving games at 9 to 12 weeks of age. Throw a toy about six feet away and encourage him to chase it. When he grabs the toy, call him back. Praise him enthusiastically when he gives it to you. If he runs away and tries to turn it into a keep-away game, stop playing. Don't chase him! Let him learn that he must play by your rules. Chasing a ball or soft flying disc can be good exercise for your puppy and it sets the stage for a sound working relationship later.

WEEKS THIRTEEN THROUGH SIXTEEN

From 13 through 16 weeks of age, your puppy will be trying to establish his position in your family pack. Consistency in enforcing the household rules is very important and everyone in the family should be doing things the same way. If he senses a soft heart or a weak link in the chain of command, he will take advantage of it.

Puppies with dominant personalities may start mounting small children or toys. This should be discouraged consistently; don't let it happen!

Socialization with other people, dogs and experiences should be continued. Make sure the experiences are positive.

WEEKS SIXTEEN TO TWENTY SIX

Sometime between 16 and 20 weeks of age many dogs go through another fear period, much like the one they had at eight weeks of age. Things the dog accepted as normal previously might become scary.

A friend's Labrador Retriever walked out into their backyard and started barking at the picnic table that had been there, in the same spot, since he was a baby. It was like he just suddenly noticed it and decided it was frightening!

During this fear stage, don't reinforce his fear. If you cuddle him and tell him, "It's okay, sweetie," he will assume that praise is for his reaction to the fear. In other words, you are praising the fear; the fear response was right! Instead, walk up to whatever is scaring him and touch it as you tell him, "Look at this." Walk him up to it if you can without frightening him too much. Help him overcome his fear instead of reinforcing it.

Every dog deserves proper training. Your Lab will thank you for it.

Many young Labs discover their protective instincts at this time, too. If your puppy Lab starts showing signs of protectiveness (growling, snarling, raised hackles) interrupt his behavior by distracting him or turning him away. If you encourage this behavior, or correct it too harshly, you will put too much emphasis on it and your puppy may continue to do it. Too much emphasis may result in overprotectiveness or fearfulness in your dog as he grows up. Instead, react with calmness and just stop it from happening.

THE TEENAGE MONTHS

The teenage months in dogs are very much like the teenage years in children. Kids in their

Exposing his belly shows that your Lab is submissive to you—and that he wants a tummy rub!

teens are feeling strong, are striving to prove their ability to take care of themselves and are trying to be independent. At the same time, they want the security of home. Those two conflicting needs seem to drive some teens (and their parents!) absolutely crazy! Dogs can be very much the same way; pushing the boundaries of their rules, testing you to see if you will enforce those rules. Many Lab owners say that during this stage of growing up, their Labs simply act "entirely too full of themselves!"

The teenage stage in Labrador Retrievers hits at any time between 8 and 14 months of age and you will know when it happens! One day you may ask your previously trained young dog to sit and he will act as if he has never heard the word before in his life! Your previously well-socialized dog may start barking or growling at other dogs, or may start pushing your children around. You may have previously taught your Lab to stay off the furniture but during this stage he may climb up there anyway, and when you tell him to get off, he will either ignore you, or in extreme cases, may even growl at you!

You will need to consistently enforce your household rules during this stage. Hopefully you have already started obedience training and if you have, make sure you practice those skills regularly. If you have not yet started training, do so now, it's not too late.

Make sure your dog regards you as his leader. You can reinforce that idea by some things you do around the house. For example, you should always go through doors first. The dominant dog, alpha wolf or leader of the pack always goes first. You should eat first, too. You should go up the stairs ahead of your dog; don't let him dash up the stairs and turn around and stare at you. If he does, he is assuming the dominant position!

Something else you can do is to give him permission to do things, even if he was going to do them anyway. For example, if he picks up his ball and is bringing it to you to throw, tell him, "Good boy to bring me your ball!" If he lies down at your feet, tell him, "Good boy to lie down!" By giving him permission and praising him, you are telling your dog that you have control.

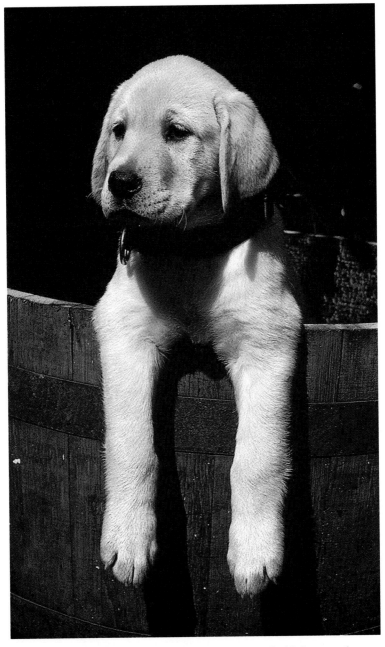

Does this look like the face of a mischief maker? Don't let his innocent face fool you—puppies can get in plenty of trouble if left unsupervised.

It is very important that you understand that your dog's adolescent behavior is natural—it is a part of growing up—and is not directed at you, personally. You must also remember that this, too, shall pass. Your Lab will grow up—someday!

GROWING UP

Labrador Retrievers are generally not considered fully mature—mentally and physically—until they are three years old. Sometimes the bitches (females) will mature a little earlier, maybe two and a half, but usually the dogs (males) take a little longer. After the teenage stage until they are grown up, your Lab may go through some different behavioral stages. There may be another fear period—usually at about a year and a half of age. Handle this one just like you did the others; don't cater to your dog's fear, just work him through it.

There may be another period of challenging—seeing if you really are the boss—at about two years of age. Treat this as you did the teenage stage; enforce the rules and praise what he does right. Sometimes there is a time when your Lab may act somewhat territorial, protective or even aggressive. Handle this just like you did when he was younger and do the same thing. Turn him away, distract him or have him do something else, but don't overreact. If you do overreact and correct him too hard, he may get the wrong message—"Wow! Something is wrong!"—and that could cause his behavior to get worse.

When your Labrador Retriever reaches the age of three years, he (or she) is generally considered to be grown up. However, "grown up" to a Lab does not necessarily mean life is serious—no way! He may be serious when he needs to be (or wants to be), but life to a Lab is still great fun! So enjoy!

Your Lab will reach maturity at about three years of age.

All About
FORMAL
Training

WHY IS TRAINING IMPORTANT?

Why did you decide to add a Labrador Retriever to your family? You probably wanted a companion, a friend and a confidant. You may have wanted a dog that could do things with you; run along the beach, catch tennis balls and hike in the mountains. To do these things your Lab will need training.

Many dog owners won't admit their dog needs training. "He does everything I ask," they say. Yet when asked specific questions about their dog's behavior, the answer changes. A trained dog is not going to jump on people, dash out the door each time it is opened or raid the trash can.

Dog owners can benefit from training, too. Dog owners learn how to teach their dog, how to

This school for Labradors is also a school for their owners. Dog owners can benefit from dog training, too.

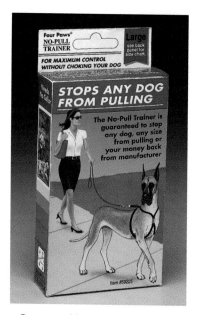

Guaranteed by the manufacturer to stop any dog, any size, any weight from ever pulling again. It's like having power steering for your dog. Photo courtesy of Four Paws.

a new light. Training will cause you to look at him a little differently, too. Dog training is not something you do to your Lab; instead it is something the two of you do together.

BONDING

Training helps build a relationship between you and your dog. This relationship is built on trust, affection and mutual respect. Training can help your dog become your best friend; a well-mannered companion who is a joy to spend time with and one who won't send your blood pressure sky-high!

praise him and how to motivate him to want to be good. They also learn how to prevent problem behavior from happening and how to correct the mistakes that do occur.

Dog training is much more than the traditional sit, down, stay, and come. Dog training means teaching your Lab that he is living in your house, not his. It means that you can establish some household rules and that he is expected to follow those rules. It will not turn your Lab into a little furry robot; but it will cause your dog to look at you in

TRAINING METHODS

Talk to a dozen dog trainers (someone who trains dogs) or dog obedience instructors (someone who teaches the dog owner how to train his or her dog) and ask them how they train and you will get a dozen different methods. Any trainer or instructor who has been in business for a period of time is going to work out a method that works for her. Each method will be based upon the trainer's personality, teaching techniques, experience and philosophy regarding dogs and dog training. Any given method may work wonderfully for one trainer but should another trainer try the same things, it may fail terribly for her.

Because there are so many different techniques, styles and methods, choosing a particular instructor can sometimes be difficult. It is important that you understand some of the different methods so that you can make a reasonable decision.

Compulsive Training

Compulsive training is regarded as a method of training that forces the dog to behave. This is usually a correction-based type of training; sometimes with quite forceful corrections. This training is often used for law enforcement and military dogs and can be quite effective for hard-driving, strong-willed dogs. In most cases, it is not the best training method for softer dogs. Many pet dog owners do not like this style of training and often feel that it is too rough.

Inducive Training

This training is exactly the opposite of compulsive training; instead of being forced to behave, the dog is induced or encouraged into the behavior. Depending upon the instructor, there are few or no corrections used. This training technique works well for many puppies, for softer dogs and sometimes for owners who dislike corrections of any kind. Unfortunately, this is not the technique for all dogs (especially all Labs) because some Labs will take advantage of the lack of corrections or discipline.

Learn the difference between inducive training and compulsive training. For many, the solution lies in the middle.

SOMEWHERE IN THE MIDDLE

The majority of trainers and instructors use a training method that is somewhere in the middle between these two techniques. An inducive technique is used when possible, while corrections are used as needed. Obviously, the range can be vast, with some trainers leaning toward more corrections, while others use as few corrections as possible.

Photo by Alan Leschinski.

Investigate the different methods of training before choosing a particular instructor. Individual dogs respond to differently to training styles.

labrador retriever

GROUP CLASSES OR PRIVATE LESSONS?

There are benefits and drawbacks to both group classes and private lessons. In group classes, the dog learns to behave around other distractions, specifically, the other dogs and people in the class. Since the world is made up of lots of things capable of distracting your dog, this can work very well for most dogs and people. In addition, group classes work much like group therapy for the dog owners. The owners can share triumphs and mishaps, and can encourage and support one another.

The drawback to group classes is that for some dogs, the distractions of the group class are too much. Some dogs simply cannot concentrate, especially in the beginning. For these dogs, a few private lessons may help enough so that the dog can join a group class later. Dogs with severe behavior problems— especially aggression towards other dogs or people—should also bypass group classes for obvious reasons.

Private lessons work well for dogs with specific problems, such as aggressive behavior. Private training is also good for dogs who are too distracted in a

Labs that are disruptive to the class will almost certainly be a problem in their home. Group training will help your Lab deal with distractions.

labrador retriever

group setting or for dog owners who are reluctant to speak up in a group class. The downfall of private training is the lack of distraction and for many instructors, the goal of private training is to get the dog and owner to the point that they can eventually join a group class.

WHAT ARE YOUR GOALS?

There are an unlimited number of things you can train your Lab to do. It's up to you to decide what you would like to do and then find a training program to help you achieve those goals. Do you want to teach your dog to be a well-behaved house dog and companion? Do you want to compete in obedience trials? Would you like to do field trial work? Perhaps you would like to share your dog with others and participate in a therapy dog program. Think about your goals and then keep them in mind as you and your dog start training.

Puppy Class

Puppy or kindergarten classes are usually for puppies over 10 weeks of age but not over 16 weeks. These classes are half training and half socialization. The puppy's owner learns how to housetrain his puppy, how to set up some household rules, and how to prevent problems from happening. The puppy learns some basic commands like sit and come. In addition, the puppy gets a chance to socialize and play with the people and puppies attending the class.

Basic Obedience Class

This class is usually for dogs over four months of age. In this class, the dogs and their owners work on the basic obedience commands, including sit, down, stay, heel, and come. Most instructors also spend time discussing problem prevention and problem solving, especially the common problems like jumping on people, barking, digging and chewing.

ADVANCED TRAINING

Advanced training classes vary in content depending upon the instructor. Some offer classes designed to teach your dog to work off leash while other emphasize hand signals or other commands. Ask the instructor what she offers.

SPORTS TRAINING

Some instructors will offer classes preparing your dog to participate or compete in dog sports. These are the classes to take if you and your Lab will be

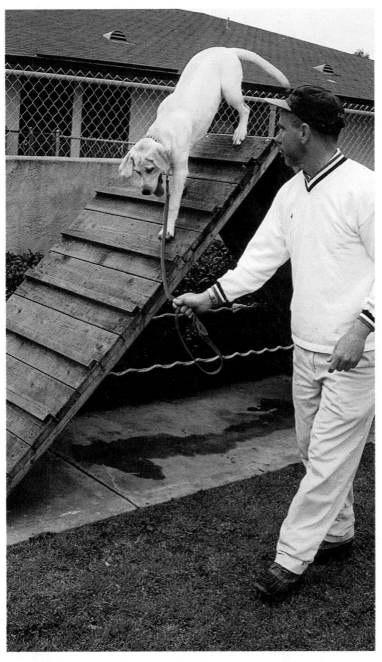

The intelligent and versatile Lab can be trained easily for any activity.

labrador retriever

competing in obedience, agility, flyball, or other dog sports.

HOW TO FIND AN INSTRUCTOR OR TRAINER

When trying to find a trainer or instructor, word-of-mouth referrals are the best place to start. Although many instructors can place an advertisement in the yellow pages or newspaper, anyone can place an ad, and a fancy ad is no guarantee of expertise. However, happy customers will demonstrate their experience with well-behaved dogs and will be glad to tell you where they received their instruction.

Have you admired a neighbor's well-behaved dog? Ask where they went for training. Call your veterinarian, local pet store or groomer and ask who they recommend. Make notes about each referral. What did people like about this instructor and what did they dislike?

Once you have a list of referrals, start calling the instructors and ask a few questions. How long has she been teaching dog obedience classes? You will want someone with experience, of course, so that she is capable of handling different situations that may arise. However, experience

When selecting an instructor or trainer, be sure to see them in action before you agree to let them train you and your Lab.

Obedience commands are not just tricks to teach your pet. They are designed to help your Lab with his behavior.

alone is not the only
qualification. Some people
that have been teaching for
years are still teaching exactly
the same way and have never
learned anything new.

Ask the instructor about
Labrador Retrievers; what does
she think of the breed? Ideally,
she should be knowledgeable of
Labs, what makes them tick and
how to train them. If she
doesn't like your breed, go
elsewhere.

Ask the instructor to
describe her training methods.
Does this sound like something
you could be comfortable with?
Ask if there are any alternative
techniques used. Not every dog
will respond to training the
same way; every instructor
should have alternative
methods ready to use.

Does the instructor belong
to any professional
organizations? The National
Association of Dog Obedience
Instructors (NADOI) and the
Association of Pet Dog
Trainers (APDT) are two of the
more prominent groups. Both
of these publish regular
newsletters to share
information, techniques, new
developments and more.
Instructors belonging to
professional organizations are
more likely to be up to date on

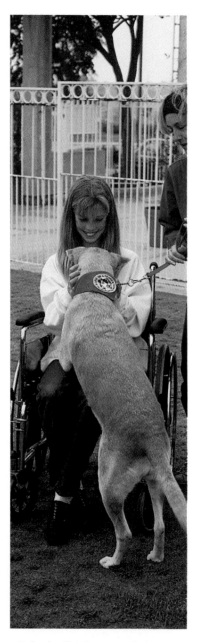

*Labrador Retrievers excel at
therapy work because of their
trainability and amiability.*

Great for the athletic dog and less active owner, these commercially designed retractable leads give the dog much more freedom when exercising in an open field or cleared area. Photo courtesy of Flexi USA, Inc.

training techniques, styles and so forth, as well as information about specific dog breeds.

Make sure, too, that the instructor will be able to help you achieve your goals. If you want to compete in obedience, make sure she can either help you towards that end goal, or can refer you to someone else who can.

After talking to the instructors, ask if you can come watch one of their classes. If the instructor says no, then cross her off your list. There should be no reason why you cannot watch one class to see if you will be comfortable with this style of training. As you watch the class, watch how she handles the students' dogs. Would you let her handle your dog? How does she relate to the students? Are people relaxed? Are they paying attention to her? Do the students seem to be making progress?

After talking to the instructors and watching a class, you should be able to make a decision as to what class you wish to attend. If you are still undecided, call the instructors back and ask a few more questions. After all, you are hiring her to provide a service and you must be comfortable with your decision.

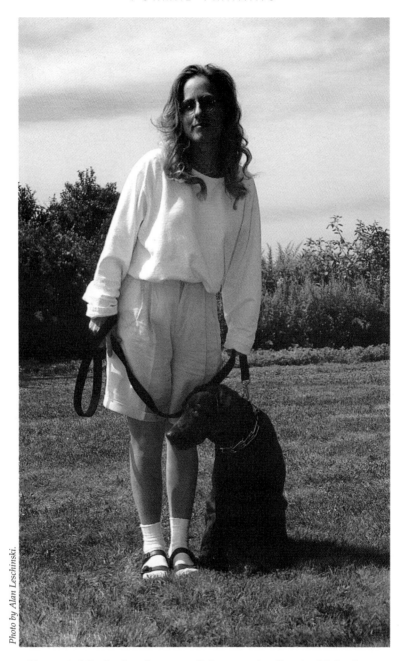

You control the destiny of your new Lab puppy. A well-trained Labrador Retriever is a joy to own.

Early
PUPPY
Training

BLANK SLATE

A puppy is like a blank slate or in this era's terms, a blank, newly formatted computer disk, ready for you to write on. What you teach the puppy in his early months will have bearing for the rest of the puppy's life. Therefore, it's important to keep in your mind a vision of what your dog will grow up to be. Although Labs are medium-sized and are not giant breeds, they are still strong, powerful dogs and you need to keep this in mind. At ten weeks of age, your Lab puppy would love to cuddle on your lap, but will you really want him to do that when he's 65 pounds of muscle, hard elbows and rough paws? By establishing some basic rules early, your puppy grows up understanding these rules. You can prevent potential problems from developing later.

CRATE TRAINING

By about five weeks of age, most puppies are starting to toddle away from their mom and littermates to relieve themselves. You can use this instinct to keep their bed clean, with the help of a crate, to help you housetrain your Lab puppy.

A crate is a plastic or wire travel cage that you can use as your Lab puppy's bed. Many new Lab owners shudder at the thought of putting their puppy in a cage, "I could never do that!" they say, "It would be like putting my children in jail!" A puppy is not a child, however, and has different needs and instincts. Puppies like to curl up in small, close places. That's

Crate training is practically a necessity for all dogs.

why they like to sleep under the coffee table or under a chair.

Because your Lab puppy does have an instinct to keep his bed clean, being confined in the crate will help him develop more bowel and bladder control. When he is confined for gradually extended periods of time, he will hold his wastes to avoid soiling his bed. It is your responsibility to make sure he is never left for too long.

The crate will also be your Lab puppy's place of refuge. If he's tired, hurt, or sick, allow him to go back to his crate to sleep or hide. If he's overstimulated or excited, put him back in his crate to calm down. Because the crate does physically confine the puppy, it can prevent some unwanted behaviors, such as chewing on electrical cords or slippers.

Introducing the Crate

Introduce your puppy to the crate by propping open the door and tossing a treat inside. As you do this, tell your puppy, "Go to bed!" and let him go in to get the treat. Let him investigate the crate and go in and out freely. When your puppy will go in after the treat and has sniffed

the crate thoroughly, offer a meal in the crate with the door propped open. The next meal can be offered in the crate and this time, close the door behind him, but let him out as soon as he has finished eating. Offer several meals in the same fashion; this is to show your puppy that the crate is a pretty neat place.

After your puppy is calm when eating in the crate, start feeding his meals back in the normal location and go back to offering him a treat or toy for going into the crate. Continue teaching him the phrase, "Go to bed!"

Don't let your puppy out of the crate for a temper tantrum. If he starts crying, screaming, throwing himself at the door or scratching at the door, correct him verbally, "No! Quiet!" or simply close the bedroom door and walk away. If you let him out for a temper tantrum, you will just teach him that temper tantrums work! Instead let him out when you are ready to let him out and when he is quiet.

Crate Location

The ideal place for the crate is in your bedroom within arm's reach of the bed. This will give him eight uninterrupted hours with you while you do nothing but sleep. In these busy times, that is quality time! Having you nearby will also give your puppy a feeling of security. If you exile him to the backyard or garage, he will be more apt to cry, whine, howl, pace, or get into trouble because of loneliness and fear. Instead, keep him close.

Having your puppy close at night will also save you some wear and tear. If he needs to go outside, you will hear him and can let him out before he has an accident. If he's restless or bored, you can rap the top of his crate and tell him to be quiet.

Your Lab will soon use his crate as a safe den in which to retreat and relax.

Your Lab will usually adapt to crate training very easily. Don't tolerate any temper tantrums if he doesn't like it—give him time!

HOUSETRAINING

One of the most common methods of training a puppy is paper training. The puppy is taught to relieve himself on newspaper and then, at some point, is retrained to go outside. Paper training teaches the puppy to relieve himself in the house. Is that really what you want your Lab to know?

Teach your puppy what you want him to know. Take him outside to the area where you want him to relieve himself and tell him, "Go potty!" (Use any command comfortable for you.)

When he has done what it is he needed to do, praise him, "Good boy to go potty!" Don't just send your Lab puppy out into the back yard and hope that he does what he needs to do; you may let him back into the house just to see him squat on the rug! You need to go with him to see that he has relieved himself, that he does so in the correct area and so that you can praise him for doing so!

PUNISHMENT

If you try to housetrain your puppy by punishing him for accidents that happen in the house, either by rubbing his nose in his mess (a commonly used correction) or by sharply scolding him, you run the risk of confusing him more than teaching him. If you correct your puppy for housetraining accidents, he may feel that going potty is what is wrong and he may start being sneaky about where he goes so that you can't catch him. You may start finding "surprises" in strange locations around the house or yard. Keep in mind that the act of relieving himself is not what is wrong; he has to do that, instead it is relieving himself in the house that is the problem.

Successful housetraining is based upon setting your puppy up for success rather than failure. Keep accidents to a minimum and praise him when he does relieve himself where he should go.

Establish a Routine

Your Lab puppy is a creature of habit; routines are very important. Housetraining is much easier if there is a set routine for eating, eliminating, playing walking, and sleeping. A workable schedule might look like this:

• **6:00 am**—Dad wakes up and takes the puppy outside. After the puppy relieves himself and dad praises him, dad fixes the puppy's breakfast, offers him water, and then takes him back outside.

• **7:00 am**—Mom goes outside to play with the puppy before getting ready for work. Just before she leaves, she brings the puppy inside and puts him in his crate and gives him a treat.

• **11:00 am**—A dog-loving neighbor who is retired comes over, lets the puppy out of his crate and takes him outside. The neighbor knows the puppy's training, so praises him when he relieves himself. He throws the Gumabone™ chew toy for the puppy, pets and cuddles him and then gives him a treat when he puts him back in his crate.

• **3:00 pm**—Daughter comes home from school, lets the puppy out into the backyard while she changes clothes. After calling her friends on the phone, she goes out back with the puppy, throws the ball, cleans up the yard a little and then takes the puppy for a walk. When they get back, she brings the puppy to her bedroom while she works on her homework.

• **6:00 pm**—Mom takes the puppy outside to go potty, praises him, and then feeds him dinner.

• **8:00 pm**—After daughter plays with the puppy, she takes him back outside.

• **11:00 pm**—Dad takes the puppy out for one more chance to go potty before going to bed.

The schedule you establish will have to work with your normal routine and lifestyle. Just keep in mind that the puppy should not remain in his crate longer than three to four hours, except at night. The puppy will need to relieve himself after eating and drinking, after exercise and playtime, and when waking up from a nap.

A workable schedule is necessary for housetraining.

labrador retriever

43

Limit the Puppy's Freedom

Many puppies do not want to take the time to go outside to go potty, especially if there are interesting things happening in the house. Those puppies will then sneak off somewhere—a back bedroom or behind the sofa—to relieve themselves. By limiting the puppy's freedom you can prevent these "accidents" from happening. Close bedrooms doors and use baby gates across hallways to keep your puppy close. If you can't keep an eye on him, put him outside or in his crate.

PRACTICE PATIENCE

New puppy owners seem to invite advice. Everyone has a method of housetraining that works better or faster and is more reliable than anyone else's method. Ignore your well-meaning friends. Lab puppies need time to grow up and develop bowel and bladder control. Establish a routine that works well for you and stick with it. If you stick with the schedule, your puppy will progress. However, don't let apparent success go to your head; don't assume he is housetrained. Too much freedom too soon will result in problems.

Household Rules

It's important to start establishing some household rules as soon as your new puppy joins your household. Your puppy, at eight to ten weeks of age, is not too young to learn and by starting early you can prevent problems from getting started. When deciding what rules you want to establish, look at your puppy, not as the baby he is now, but rather the adult he will grow up to be. You may not mind if your Lab puppy is on the couch now but are you going to want him up there when he's full grown? Do you want him jumping on people? A full-grown Lab is powerful enough to knock over kids, senior citizens and even adults not paying attention.

Some common household rules might include teaching your puppy not to jump on people, to behave when guests come over, to stay out of the kitchen and not to chew on inappropriate things. In addition, you might want to teach the puppy to leave the kids' toys alone, to ignore dirty clothes and to stay off the furniture.

To teach your puppy what is allowed and what is not, you must be very clear with your commands and corrections.

Either something is right or it is wrong. When the puppy picks up his toy instead of your slippers, praise him, "Good boy to play with your toy!" When he picks up your slipper, correct him, "No! That's not yours!" Take the slipper away and then give him one of his toys, "Here this is your toy! Let him know what is wrong, then follow it by showing him what he can do instead and praise him when he does it.

ACCEPTING THE LEASH

All dogs need to accept the restraints of a leash and this can be hard for some puppies. If your Lab puppy is frightened by the leash as a baby, he may resent the leash for the rest of his life. Therefore you want to introduce the leash calmly and positively.

Soon after you bring your puppy home, put a soft nylon or cotton buckle collar on him. Make sure it's loose enough to slip over his head should he get tangled up with something (as Lab puppies are known to do!) After a day or two, when he is no longer scratching at the collar, attach a leash to the collar and let him drag it around the house for 10 or 15 minutes, while you watch him to make sure it

Your Lab will become used to his collar and leash in no time.

Once he is accustomed to walking on his leash, your Lab can accompany you anywhere.

Photos by Alan Leschinski.

doesn't tangle on something. While the puppy is dragging the leash, he will step on the leash, feel the tug on his neck and just generally get used to the feel of it.

After two or three sessions of dragging the leash, you can teach your puppy to follow you when you have the leash in hand. Have a few pieces of a soft treat you know he likes, such as a hot dog or cheese. Let him sniff the treat and then back away while you verbally encourage him, "Let's go! Good boy!" When he follows you for a few feet, stop, praise him and let him have a bite of the treat. Labs are the original, proverbial food hounds and training with treats for these dogs makes training much easier!

Repeat the exercise two or three times and quit for this session. Reward your puppy by throwing the tennis ball a few times. After two or three training sessions like this, start making it more challenging by backing away from your puppy faster or by adding turns or zigzags. If he balks or acts confused, stop and go back to the simple back away again until he understands.

PRAISE
Never stop the training session when your Lab puppy is confused. Instead, always stop the training session on a high note. Do something you know he can do and do well, then stop, praise him enthusiastically and play ball with him for a few minutes.

INTRODUCING THE CAR

Many puppies are frightened by riding in the car because the car took them away from mom and their littermates and the car takes them to the veterinarian's office where scary things happen. You don't want this idea to blossom, though, you want your puppy to understand that riding in the car can be a good thing.

Start by lifting your puppy into the car and handing him a good treat. As soon as he has eaten the treat, lift him down and walk away. Repeat that sporadically over several days. Then lift him into the car, give him a treat, let him eat it and let him explore the car a little. After he has sniffed a little, give him another treat, let him eat it and lift him out of the car. Continue this type of training for a week or more, depending upon how nervous your puppy is about the car. When your puppy is expecting a treat in the car, then take his crate, put it in the car and strap it down so that it won't bounce around or go flying in an emergency situation. Put your puppy in his crate, give him a treat and close the crate door and the car door. Start the engine, back the car out of the driveway and then drive back up to the house. Give your puppy a treat and let him out of the crate. The next time, drive down the street and back, then around the block. Increase the time and distance of the drives very gradually.

Keep in mind that you want your puppy to anticipate good things in the car, not scary things. Your dog will have a lifetime of car rides ahead of him and life will be much nicer if he can enjoy the rides.

SOCIAL HANDLING

Your puppy cannot care for himself; you must be able to brush him, pull burrs and foxtails out of his coat, clean his ears, and trim his nails. Unfortunately, your Lab puppy doesn't understand that cleaning his ears is necessary and he may struggle and fight when you try to do these things. The social handling exercise will help teach your puppy to accept your care.

Social handling will help your Lab to accept your care.

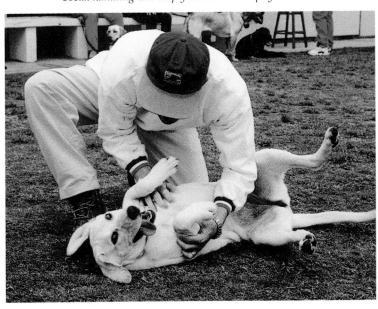

labrador retriever

Sit on the floor and have your puppy lie down between your legs. He can lie on his back or his side and can get comfortable. Start by giving him a slow, easy tummy rub; the idea here is to relax him. If he starts to wiggle or struggle, gently restrain him with one hand as you massage him with the other.

When the puppy is no longer struggling, start giving him a massage. Start at his neck and ears and gently massage the muscles. Work down his neck to his shoulders, down each front leg to the paw. Touch the paw gently but firmly (some dogs are ticklish) and touch each toenail. Go back to his body and massage the back, the ribcage and the hips. Work down the back legs just like you did his front legs. And then give his tail a little massage as well.

Once your puppy has learned to enjoy this handling, you can—during the massage—check his ears and clean them when needed, brush him, check for fleas or ticks, trim his toenails, comb out burrs or even medicate him when necessary.

CALMING DOWN

Social handling can even be used to calm an excited or overstimulated puppy. If you let your puppy in from the backyard and he is just bouncing off the walls with excitement and energy, you have a couple of choices. If you try to correct the puppy, he will probably just get more excited. However, if you grab him and lay him down, and start massaging him, he will relax. In addition, you are giving him the attention he wants and needs from you.

You should be able to have your Lab lie down and rest quietly when you have to check him for fleas or examine him for any other reason.

labrador retriever

The Basic
OBEDIENCE
Commands

TEACHING YOUR LABRADOR RETRIEVER

Teaching your Lab is a process. Unfortunately you cannot simply tell your dog to sit and expect him to do it. First of all, until he has been taught what the word "sit" means, it is simply an unknown sound. To confuse training even more, he has no idea why you want him to sit nor does he know why it is so important to you. Therefore, teaching becomes a process.

You want to show your dog what it is you want him to do. Help shape him into the sit if that is what you are teaching, or move him off the furniture if that is your focus. Then, as you are helping him, teach him the word, "Sit" or "Off the furniture." Praise him when he does it right, even if you have helped him, "Good boy to sit!" or "Good boy to get off the furniture."

Praise him every time he does something right. Your dog will work harder and do more for you when you use a lot of praise. That doesn't mean that you should give undeserved praise; even your dog can figure that out. Instead, give enthusiastic praise when he makes an effort and does something right for you.

> ### DON'T PRACTICE INCORRECT BEHAVIOR
> Interrupt incorrect behavior or actions as your dog is thinking about it or starts to move. If you have asked him to sit and he does, but then starts to sniff and lean as if he is going to get up, interrupt him, "Don't do it!" When he looks at you, tell him, "That's good to sit!"

Do not correct your dog for not cooperating until you are sure he understands what it is you are asking him to do. Once he understands and is willing to do it, then when he chooses not to, you can correct him with a verbal correction or a quick snap and release of the leash. Use ONLY as much correction as needed to get his attention and NO MORE. With corrections, less is better!

Interruptions and corrections will not teach your dog; they

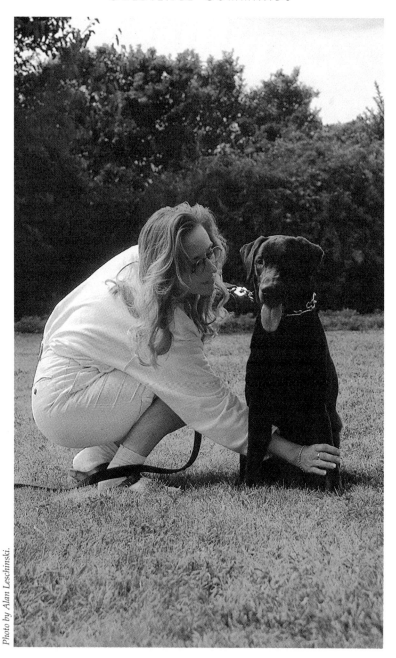

Photo by Alan Leschinski.

The sit command is absolutely necessary for every Lab. Be sure to lavish praise during the sit training.

are used only to stop—at that moment—undesirable behavior or actions. Your dog learns much more when you reward his good behavior. So stop what you don't want, but lavishly praise what you do want!

Timing is vitally important as you teach your dog. Make sure you praise him as he is doing something right and interrupt or correct him as he is making a mistake.

BE FAIR

Make sure you are very clear as to what you want from your dog. Remember, to your dog something is either right or wrong; it's not partially right or partially wrong. Be fair with your demands, your praise and your corrections.

SIT AND RELEASE

The sit is the foundation command for everything else you will teach your Lab. When your Lab learns to sit and sit still, he is also learning to control himself. Learning self control is a very hard lesson for many young Labs; being still is simply not in their genetic code! However, your Lab can learn to control himself and the sit is the place to start.

The sit is also the foundation command for many other exercises, including the down and wait, as well as many advanced obedience commands. The sit is also great around the house. Your Lab cannot jump up on people for petting if he is sitting. He cannot knock his food bowl

Praise in a soft voice is wonderful, but a tasty treat is probably appreciated more.

out of your hand at dinner time if he's sitting. You can fasten his leash to his collar more easily if he is sitting still. It's a useful command!

There two methods to teach your Lab to sit. Some methods work better for one dog than they do the other, so try both and see which will be better. Hold your Lab's leash in your left hand and have some treats in your right hand. Tell your Lab to sit as you move your right hand (and the treats) from his nose over his head towards his tail. He will lift his head to follow your hand and will sit in response to that movement. As he sits,

praise him, "Good boy to sit!" Pet him while he's in the sitting position, give him a treat and have him hold the sit until you pat him on the shoulder to release him, "Release!" We want this release command to tell your dog that he is finished with that particular exercise and can move. You will be using the release with several different exercises.

If your dog is too excited by treats to concentrate on sitting, or if he spins around in place to get the treat instead of sitting, then try the second technique. Tell your Lab to sit as you put your right hand on the front of his chest as your

Shaping the Lab into a proper sit.

labrador retriever

Two more steps in shaping the Lab into a proper sit.

left hand slides down his back to his rump and you gently shape him into a sit. Praise him for sitting, pet him quietly, and do not allow him to pop back up. If he does, shape him back into position. If he is very wiggly, keep your hands on him as you praise him for sitting, then, with your hands on him, you can gently restrain him so that he cannot pop back up. When you are ready for him to move from the sit, pat him on the shoulder and tell him, "Release!" Don't get into the habit of repeating your commands. If you tell your dog to sit three or four times, which one should he listen to? You are not teaching him sit

by repeating it, but you are teaching him that he doesn't have to listen to you. Is that really what you want him to learn? Instead, give each command only once and then help your dog to succeed. Tell him to sit, wait a heartbeat to allow him to do it and if he doesn't, help him do it.

DOWN

The down exercise continues one of the lessons the sit exercise started; that of self control. It is hard for many young, bouncy Labs to control their own actions but it's a lesson that all must learn. Teaching and practicing the down teaches your Lab to lie down and be still.

Start with your Lab in a sit. Rest one hand gently on his shoulders and have a treat in the other hand. Let him smell the treat and then tell him, "Dog, lie down," as you take the treat straight down to the ground in front of his front paws. As he follows the treat to the ground, use your hand on his shoulders to encourage him to lie down. Praise him, give him the treat, have him hold the position for a few moments and then release in the same manner that you did from the sit. Pat him on the shoulder and tell him, "Release!"

If your Lab looks at the treat as you make the signal but doesn't follow the treat to the ground, simply scoop his front legs up and forward and lay him down. The rest of the exercise is the same.

As your Lab learns what "lie down" means, you can have him hold it for a few seconds longer before you release him but do not step away from him. Stay next to him and if you need to, keep a hand on his shoulder to encourage him to remain down.

The down command can be difficult for the energetic Lab puppy to master, but with practice, he soon will obey.

Photo by Alan Leschinski.

STAY

When you taught your Lab to sit and to lie down, you taught him to move into those positions and to hold still until you released him. The stay command continues those exercises by teaching your dog to continue to hold still for gradually increasing times as you move away from him. Eventually your Lab will be able to hold the sit or down stay for several minutes (longer in the down) and when you are a distance away, maybe even in another room.

Start by having your Lab sit. With the leash in your left hand, use the leash to put a slight bit of pressure backwards (towards his tail) as you tell him, "Dog, stay." At the same time, use your right hand to give your dog a signal that will mean stay—an open hand gesture with the palm towards your dog's face. Take one step away and at the same time, release the pressure on the leash. If your Lab moves towards you, gets up or lies down, tell him "No" (so that he understands he has made a mistake) and put him back into position. Repeat the exercise. After a few seconds—and a few seconds only—step back to your dog and praise him. Don't let him

Phot o by Alan Leschinski.

This owner gives her Lab the hand signal for the stay command.

move from the position until you give him the release command.

You can use the same process to teach your dog to stay in the down position. Have him sit, then lie down. Give him the verbal command to stay and the hand signal while putting slight pressure backwards on the leash. Step one step away as you release pressure on the leash. If he moves, tell him "No" and put him back into position. After a few seconds, go back to him, praise him, and then release him.

With the stay commands, you always want to go back to your dog to release him. Don't release him from a distance or call him to come from the stay. If you do either of these, your dog will be much less reliable on the stay; he will continue to get up from the stay or will start to anticipate the release from a distance. When teaching the stay, you want your dog to understand that stay means "Hold this position until I go back to you and release you." No confusion and no questions asked.

As your dog learns the stay command, you can increase the time he holds the stay.

However, make sure you increase the time very gradually. If your dog is making a lot of mistakes, moving often, you are either asking your dog to hold the stay too long or your dog doesn't understand the command yet. In either case, go back and teach the command from the beginning, increasing the time you ask him to hold the stay very gradually.

Increase the distance you move away from your dog just as gradually. Again, if your dog is making a lot of mistakes,

As your Lab learns the stay command, you can increase the time he holds the stay, as well as the distance between you and your dog.

labrador retriever

Photo by Alan Leschinski.

This chocolate Labrador is demonstrating the down/stay with a hand signal.

make sure he understands what you are asking him to do. Then, increase the distance one step away at a time.

Once your Lab understands the stay command and you know that he understands it, you can start correcting mistakes. As has been mentioned before (and will be mentioned again!) young Labs are wiggly, bouncy creatures that have a hard time holding still. Self control is a skill that must be learned. If your Lab is having a hard time holding still, keep the stay short in time and distance. Correct excess movement with a sharp verbal correction and a snap and release of the leash. When your dog does hold the stay, especially when he has been having a hard time, praise him enthusiastically!

The sit-stay sequence must be thoroughly learned before it can be deemed reliable. Never let your Lab off his leash until you are sure he is properly trained.

SOCIAL GRACES OF THE STAY COMMAND

When your Lab has learned the basics on the stay, start using the down stay around the house. Have your dog down stay while you are eating so that he isn't begging under the table or stealing food from the kids. Have him do a down stay when guests come over so he isn't jumping all over your guests. There are a lot of practical uses for this command; just look at your normal routine and see where they can work for you and then use them.

WATCH ME

The watch me exercise is a very useful command that teaches your Lab to ignore distractions and focus on you. This will be particularly useful when you and your dog are out in public and he gets excited by children playing, dogs barking or birds flying overhead.

Start by having your dog sit in front of you. With the leash in your left hand, have a treat in your right hand. Let your dog smell the treat and then take it up to your chin as you tell him, "Dog, watch me!" When his eyes follow your hand to your face and he looks at you, praise him,

"Good boy to watch me!" Give him the treat and release him from the sit. This is a particularly hard exercise for many young Labs so teach him first in the house with few distractions. Make sure your dog can do it and understands it well before moving on to the next step.

When he will watch you while you practice in the house, then move outside where there are more distractions. If he knows the command and ignores you, take his chin in your left hand as you give the signal with your right. Help him to look at you. If he still struggles

This Lab watches his owner for his next command.

Establishing eye contact with your Labrador is very important when training your dog.

against you, use a verbal correction. When he looks back at you, praise him.

When your dog will watch you outside with a few distractions you can move on to the next training step. Start with your dog sitting in front of you, give him the command, "Watch me," and then start walking backwards. Encourage him to follow you and watch you at the same time. After six steps (or so) stop and have him sit, then praise him enthusiastically! After a few tries, back up a little farther,

then add turns and zigzags. Make it challenging and when he can watch you, make the praise worthwhile, tell him what a wonderful dog he is!

HEEL

When your Lab can watch you while you walk backwards, then you are ready to teach the heel. Heel will mean, "Walk with me, by my left side, with your neck and shoulders by my left leg. You will pay attention to me and walk as I do; slow, fast, normal, left turns, right turns and anything else." Obviously, this is a complicated exercise. However, if your Lab is watching well, it won't be too hard.

To first start it, practice a watch me exercise as you have been doing it; backing away from your dog. When he is following you well and paying attention, simply turn your body—as you are walking—so that you and your dog end up walking forward together with him on your left side. Picture this in your mind—you are backing away from your dog, your dog is facing you, following you. Back to your dog's right as you continue walking. You and your dog should be facing the same direction with your dog on your left. This is the heel. When you stop, have your dog sit.

If while you are walking, and your dog starts to pull forward, simply back away from him and encourage him to follow you again. If you need to, use the leash to make sure he follows you quickly. Praise him when he does. When his attention is back on you, turn into the heel position again. Don't be upset if you have to back away a few times. In fact, the more you do it, the better. Your

Photo by Alan Leschinski.

In the heel command, the dog must never lose sight of your legs. Don't let him get ahead of you!

dog will pay more attention to you if he's not quite sure where you will be going.

When your dog is walking with you nicely, then you can start eliminating the backing away. Start the heel with your dog sitting on your left side, tell him, "Watch me! Dog, heel!" and start walking. Praise him when he's walking nicely with you. If he starts to pull, you can correct him, "Dog, no pull!" However, if he is intent upon pulling or is distracted, simply back away from him and turn him away from whatever is distracting him.

COME

With a Treat

The come command is one of the most important commands your Labrador Retriever needs to know. Not only is the come important around the house and yard, but should he be out in front of your house, the come could save him from dashing into the street and getting hit by a car. If you take him out to run, or you decide to do field or gun dog work with him, he must have a good, reliable come.

Because the come is so important, you will use two different techniques for teaching the come. The first method will use food treats to teach your Lab that the come is fun and will result in a treat; something near and dear to all Labs! Take a small plastic container, like a small margarine container, and put some dog food kibble in it so that it makes a nice plastic rattling sound. Then, have some treats in hand that you know your dog really likes— something special. Shake the container and ask your dog if he wants a treat, using the word he already knows for treat, such as cookie, biscuit or bone. "Dog, do you want a cookie?" Then pop a treat in his mouth. This, combined with shaking the container, teaches your dog that the sound of the container equals a treat. Do this for several days until your dog comes running whenever he hears the container rattling.

At that point, you can shake the container and say, "Dog, cookie! Come!" This builds a relationship between the words cookie and come. After a few days, drop the word cookie altogether and simply shake the container, say, "Dog, come!" and pop a treat in his mouth.

Practice this command two or three times per training session, several times a day. Don't do it too many times in one session or it will lose its appeal. However, you do need to practice it a lot so that the dog reacts to it automatically, without even thinking about what he's doing.

Some people have reservations about this technique, worrying that their dog will not come to them when they don't have a treat. First of all, you will be using two different techniques to teach your Lab to come for that express reason. Later, when your dog is coming reliably every time you call him, you will be able to get rid of the treats, although it is important to use them as long as you need them. In addition, this technique— when taught properly—can produce such a

Treats are excellent motivators when teaching the come command.

wonderful, strong reliable come that it is worth all your efforts.

With the Long Line

The second method will teach your dog to come when he's a little farther away from you. It will also help teach your Lab to come to you on those instances when you don't have the treat container.

With this technique, you will need a 20- to 30-foot length of cotton clothesline rope. Don't use nylon, that is too rough on your hands. Fasten the rope to your dog's collar and let him go play. When he is distracted by a bird or his toys, call him, "Dog, come!" If he comes to you right away, praise him enthusiastically. If he does not come directly to you, do NOT call him again. Simply pick up the rope, back away from him, and using the rope, make him come to you. Now the key to this is to verbally praise him even if you have to drag him in to you. The come has to be positive; if he thinks he's going to get into trouble by coming to you, he won't come at all. So you have to praise him. Let the long line be the bad guy.

After you have praised him, release him and let him go play

again. In a few minutes repeat the exercise all over again. Practice this in the back yard and in the front yard, even in the house if he plays keep away in the house. Teach your dog that he must come to you the first time you call him, every time you call him.

Don't allow your Lab freedom off leash in an unfenced area until he is well-trained, grown up and mentally mature enough to handle that responsibility. Many dog owners let their dogs off leash much too soon and the dog learns that he can run away from them or play keep away; staying just out of reach. Each time he does this,

he learns that he can and there is nothing you can do to change his mind. Therefore, leave him on leash or on a long line.

USE IT OR LOSE IT!

The best way to make this obedience training work for you and your Labrador is to use it. Training is not just for training sessions, it is for daily life. Incorporate the training into your daily routine. Have him lie down and stay during meals or when company comes over. Have him sit and stay at doorways so that he isn't dashing out open doors. Use these commands and make them a part of your life. They will work better that way.

Keeping your dog on leash when teaching him to come to you ensures that he will obey the command. Remember to praise him no matter how he comes to you.

Photo by Alan Leschinski.

labrador retriever

Advanced
TRAINING
and Dog Sports

One of the great things about dog training is that you are never finished; there is always more you can teach your dog. Would you like your Lab to behave himself off leash? You can teach him that. Wouldn't teaching him to recognize and respond to some hand signals be fun? It is. Your dog can learn hand signals for down, sit, stand, stay and more, including directions left and right.

to respond to the sit, lie down, stay, and heel (on leash) with one command and very few corrections. Ideally, he should also come to you when you call (off leash in the house or fenced yard) using the shaker and a verbal command. If your dog is still having some trouble with the basics, work on those some more before going on to these commands.

HAND SIGNALS

When you start teaching your Lab hand signals, use a treat in your hand to get his attention and use the verbal command he already knows to help him understand what you want. As he responds better and starts to show some understanding of the command, you can then make the verbal command softer, and eventually stop saying it.

The difficult part of teaching your dog hand signals is that in the beginning, he may not understand that there is some significance in your motions. After all, people move their hands constantly, especially when they are talking, and your

DAILY USES

Some people teach advanced obedience commands for competition or other dog sports, which we'll talk more about later in this chapter. But some of these commands are great for your daily life with your dog. For example, if your dog responds to hand signals, you can give him the signal to go lie down and stay while you are talking on the telephone. That way you won't interrupt your conversation.

Before you start teaching any of these commands, make sure he is proficient at his basic commands. He should be able

You can eliminate the tugging and tearing of your dog's coat in the detangling process. Your dog will appreciate it, and his coat is less likely to be split or torn. Photo courtesy of Wahl, USA.

dog may not realize that those motions could mean something. Also, for hand signals to work, your dog must be watching you!

Down

When you taught your Lab to lie down by taking a treat to the ground in front of his feet, you were starting to teach him a hand signal. Granted, he was watching the treat in your hand, but he was also getting used to seeing your hand take the treat there. That motion of your hand is a signal; a command that can mean the same thing as your verbal command, "Down." Continue using the treat in the beginning; don't get rid of the treat until you are sure that he knows the signal and is

following the hand signal reliably.

Start teaching him by practicing the down with the signal as you taught him earlier. Have him sit, tell him, "Down" and take the treat to the ground in front of him. When he's down, praise him and release him. If he's doing this well, with no hesitation, give him the signal and delay your whispered verbal command by a couple seconds. If he lies down for your signal, praise him enthusiastically! If he waits for your verbal command, try it again with more emphasis on the signal.

When he can follow the signal with no verbal command, start making it more challenging. Continue to have him sit, but

Photo by Alice Pantfoeder.

Hand signals in conjunction with verbal commands are very effective when training your Labrador Retriever.

stand in front of him and then signal him to lie down. Walk a leash length's away and try it. Try it from across the room. Remember to praise him enthusiastically when he follows your signal and lies down.

Sit

If you were able to teach your Lab to sit using the treat above his nose, you were starting to teach him a signal that means sit. If you weren't able to use that technique, don't worry, he can still learn a sit signal.

With your Lab on the leash held in your left hand, have a treat in your right hand, and standing in front of him, take the treat from his nose up to your left shoulder so that your forearm is up and across your chest. At the same time, tell him, "Dog, sit" in a soft voice. If he hesitates, give him a jiggle of the leash and collar. If he refuses, tell him to sit again and snap and release the leash. When he sits, praise him, give him the treat, release him and try it again.

Stay

As you taught your Lab the stay command earlier, you were again introducing him to a hand signal. When you said, "Dog, stay" and put your open

labrador retriever

67

palm in front of his nose, that was a hand signal. In fact, this signal is so obvious, your dog will probably obey it right away with little extra training. Try it by having your dog sit, then give him the stay signal without a verbal command and see what happens. Did he hold it? If he did, go back to him and praise him. If he didn't, put him back where he started, give him the signal again, and quietly tell him to stay.

Come

The come signal will start with your right hand and arm straight out to your side at shoulder height. Bring it around to your chest as if you were reaching out to get your dog and bringing him to you. Finish it by making the sit signal; up and across your chest, so that when your Lab comes dashing to you, he will see the sit signal and sit in front of you.

Start teaching it by having the come shaker in your right hand and shake it slightly as you make the arm signal and quietly tell your dog to come. You may also need to quietly tell your dog to sit as you finish with the sit command. He isn't used to watching more than one command at a time. When he comes and sits,

praise him enthusiastically and give him a treat.

Watch your dog and when he seems to understand the signal, take away the shaker and practice the signal with a quiet verbal command. Continue to pop a treat in his mouth when he does come. Gradually eliminate the verbal command but continue to praise and reward him for coming to you.

USING THE HAND SIGNALS

When your dog has a good understanding of the hand signals, you can start putting them together and using them in groups as part of your training sessions. Have your Lab come, sit, lie down, and then come again. Praise him enthusiastically and reward him with a treat. Or rearrange the order; have him lie down, then come back up to a sit, then come and lie down again. Challenge your training skills and his learning and attention skills.

OFF-LEASH CONTROL

One of the biggest mistakes people make with their dogs is to take them off the leash too soon. When your dog is off leash, you have very little (or no) control and your dog will learn very quickly that he can get away from you and there's nothing you can do about it. Labs are very inquisitive dogs and love to explore. More than one Lab has gotten so involved in his exploring that he has forgotten he should have been paying attention to his owner.

Before he is allowed total off-leash freedom (outside of your house or fenced in yard) you need to make sure that his training is sound. That means he understand the basic commands and responds to them reliably.

Your Labrador Retriever must also be mentally mature enough to handle the responsibility of off-leash freedom. Mentally mature means that he is through the adolescent challenging stage of growing up. Most Labs are not mentally adults until they are two and a half or three years old, some even older. Until then they are still very puppylike and don't take anything seriously. There's nothing wrong with this; many people love puppies, even big puppies! However, puppies do not have the concentration, responsibility and seriousness to be allowed off-leash freedom.

The Long Leash and the Come

The long leash that was introduced in the section on teaching the come command is a good training tool for teaching off-leash control. Earlier, you used the long leash to teach your dog to come to you when he was a distance (but within reach of the long leash) from you. Review that training session by putting your Lab on the long leash and while holding one end of it, let him go play. When he is distracted and not paying attention to you, call him to come and back away from him so that he gets a chance to chase you. (The chase is exciting to most dogs and this will make the come more exciting.) If he doesn't immediately start to come to you, use the long leash to give him a snap and release. If he is still ignoring you, reel him in like a fish on a fishing pole. When he gets to you, either under his own power or yours, you must praise him. The come must be rewarded; however, if he comes to you voluntarily, the praise should be much more enthusiastic!

Heel

In most public places dogs are required to be on leash; however, the off-leash heel is a required part of obedience competition. It has some practical uses, too. If your Lab is well trained, you can tell him to heel and walk him to your car or the mailbox without worrying about a leash. What happens if you are out on a walk and the leash breaks? Or his collar? It's happened before and will happen again. If your dog can heel by your side without a leash and collar, you won't need to panic.

Hook two leashes up to your dog's collar; his normal leash and a second, very light-weight leash. Do a watch me with treats, then practice his heel work; having him walk nicely with you as you walk slow, fast, normal and turn corners. Stop and have him sit while you praise him. Then reach down and unhook his regular leash and toss it to the ground in front of him. If he bounces up, thinking he's free, correct him, "I didn't release you!" and bring him back to the sit position. Hook his regular leash back up and repeat the exercise.

When he sits still for the leash to be tossed to the ground, continue by telling him to heel and then practice his heel work as you did with both leashes. Stop, have him sit, put the regular leash back on and repeat the whole thing again. Go back and forth between one leash and two so much that he won't remember what he has on. Repeat this over several training sessions. Remember to use the watch me command with treats to help keep his attention on you.

When he is to the point of behaving himself regardless of the leash or leashes, then take off the second leash. Fold his regular leash up and tuck it under his collar over his shoulder blades, so that it is on his back. Practice his heel work. If he makes a mistake or tries to take advantage, grab the leash on his back.

DOG SPORTS

Have you discovered that you like training your Labrador Retriever? A lot of Lab owners start with puppy or basic training and discover that it is a lot more fun than they expected. For those who like training, there are a lot of dog sports that you and your Lab can participate in. Some are just for fun. Others are recreational, others are competitive and a couple are in the service of people.

Expect (and demand) the same quality of work off leash that you expect when he's working on leash. Don't make excuses for mistakes off leash. Once your dog has mastered off-leash control, there is a whole new world waiting for you both; dog sports!

Conformation Competition

The American Kennel Club and the United Kennel Club all

award conformation championships to purebred dogs. The requirements vary between the registries but basically the championship is earned when a purebred dog competes against other dogs of its breed and wins. When competing, the judge compares each dog to the standard for that breed (What is the perfect Labrador Retriever?) and chooses the dog that most closely represents this written description.

This is a very simplistic explanation, however. If you feel that your Lab might be a good conformation candidate, write to either the American Kennel Club or the United Kennel Club and ask for information about competing in conformation. You will also want to do some reading on your breed and compare your dog to the written standard. You may also wish to attend a

In conformation, your Lab is judged on how closely he conforms to the breed standard.

few dog shows in your area and watch the conformation competition to see if this is a sport you would be interested in.

Obedience Competition

Obedience competition is a team sport; you and your dog. There are set exercises that must be performed a certain way and both you and your dog are judged as to your ability to perform those exercises. Many, many Labradors have done very well in obedience.

Both the American Kennel Club and the United Kennel Club sponsor obedience competition. There are also independent obedience tournaments—not associated with either the AKC or the UKC—held all over the country.

Obedience competition.

Again, you may wish to attend a local dog show and watch the obedience competition first. If this is something you would like to do, write to the AKC or UKC for a copy of their obedience competition rules and regulations. You will also need to find a dog trainer in your area experienced in obedience competition training to help you. There are also many books on the market that can help you prepare for competition.

Canine Good Citizen

The Canine Good Citizen program was introduced by the American Kennel Club in an effort to promote and reward responsible pet ownership. During a Canine Good Citizen test, the dog and owner must complete a series of ten exercises, including sitting still for petting and grooming, walking nicely on a leash, sit, down, stay, and come. Upon completion of all ten exercises, the dog is awarded the title CGC.

For more information, contact the American Kennel Club or a dog trainer in your area.

Flyball

Is your Lab, like so many others, absolutely tennis ball crazy? If so, then flyball is the sport for you. In flyball, dogs compete on a team. The dogs race over a course of hurdles, hit a machine that tosses a tennis ball, grab the ball and race back over the hurdles. The team that finishes first, wins.

AGILITY

Agility is a fast growing and popular dog sport that combines a grand prix jumping event with an obstacle course. The dog must run through, jump over and otherwise complete a series of obstacles in a set order. The dog is judged both by his manner of completing the course (safety is stressed) and how quickly he ran.

The American Kennel Club, United Kennel Club and the United States Dog Agility Association sponsor agility competitions; write to them for rules and competition information.

This Lab negotiates the cat walk in an agility competition.

Flyball has become so popular in some parts of the country that tournaments are held on a regular basis with numerous teams competing.

If your Lab is tennis ball crazy, contact the North American Flyball Association for competition rules.

Hunting, Retrieving and Field Events

These sports are made for Labrador Retrievers. This breed is the breed of choice for many sportsmen in a variety of field and gun dog events.

There are a variety of organizations that sponsor hunting and field trials. The American Kennel Club and United Kennel Club sponsor events as do several independent groups. Rules and regulations vary, as do the field conditions. Different types of retrieves are required, in heavy brush, open brush, or in water. Field trials are so popular that tests and tournaments are held all over the country, even in populated areas where you might not expect this type of sport.

Temperament Test

The American Temperament Test Society was founded as a

Photo by Karen J. Taylor.

The breed of choice for many sportsmen, the Labrador excels in hunting and retrieving.

GET CERTIFIED

The Labrador Retriever Club of America also offers a Working Certificate Program to provide a means of acknowledging the breed's natural abilities. For more information, contact Dr. Pet Crockett, PO Box 80081, Austin, TX 78727.

For more information about hunting, field and retriever tests, contact the American Kennel Club, Hunting Retriever Club or the North American Hunting Retriever Association.

means a means to provide breeders and trainers with a means of uniformly evaluating a dog's temperament. By using a standardized test, with each dog being tested in exactly the same manner, the test could be used as a means of comparing and evaluating

You want a Lab that can be trusted with children. A temperament test is well advised.

our dogs are to us, researchers have now admitted that dogs are good medicine. Therapy dogs provide love, affection, warmth, a sense of touch and motivation to people who need it. Therapy dogs visit hospitals, nursing homes, day care centers, and hospices.

Scent Work

Does your Lab use his nose to discover the world? Most do. Labrador Retrievers have wonderful scenting abilities and have been used in many working situations because of this talent. Labs have been trained to detect flammable substances and participate in arson investigations. Labs are used to find bombs, illegal drugs and even illegal foods coming into the country from abroad or over the border. A US Customs Service Lab named Snag has intercepted millions of dollars of contraband.

potential breeding stock, future working dogs or simply as a way for dog owners to see how their dog might react in any given situation.

For more information about the test and a schedule of tests in your area, write to the American Temperament Test Society.

Therapy Dogs

Although dog owners have always known how important

Exercising your Lab is a necessity...it won't hurt you either.

Problem
PREVENTION
and Solving

Most of the behaviors that you might consider a problem—such as digging, barking, jumping on people, chewing and so on—aren't problems to your Labrador Retriever. Your dog digs because the dirt smells good, because the weather is hot and he wants to lie in some cooler dirt, or because you have gophers that he would like to play with. All of the things that you consider problems, your Lab is doing for a reason. However, that doesn't mean that there is nothing you can do. Most problem behavior can be worked with and if it cannot be stopped entirely, it can be controlled or prevented.

TRAINING

Training can play a big part in controlling problem behavior. A fair yet firm training program teaches your dog that you are in charge, that he is below you in the family, and should reinforce his concept of you as a kind, calm, caring leader. You can also use your training skills to teach your dog what is acceptable and what is not.

WHAT CAN YOU DO?

Health Problems

Some experts feel that 20 percent of all behavior problems commonly seen are caused by health related problems. A bladder infection commonly causes housetraining problems. Medications can cause behavior changes. Sometimes thyroid problems can cause a behavior problem, so can hyperactivity, hormone imbalances and a variety of other health problems. If you have some concerns as to your dog's physical health, make an appointment with your veterinarian.

Nutrition

Nutrition often plays a part in problem behavior. If your dog is not eating a good quality food, or if he isn't digesting his food properly, his body may be missing some vital nutrients. If your Lab is chewing on rocks or wood, is eating the stucco off the side of your house, is grazing on the plants in your backyard, or is eating dirt, he may have a nutritional problem. Some dogs

One of the fundamentals of good health throughout your dog's life is a sound, healthy diet. Photo courtesy of Nutro Products, Inc.

EXERCISE

Exercise is just as important for your Lab as it is for you. It works the body, uses up excess energy, relieves stress and clears the mind. How much exercise and what type depends upon your dog. A fast-paced walk might be enough exercise for a senior Lab but a young, healthy adult Labrador Retriever will need a good run or a fast paced game of ball. Maybe even a fast paced game of ball after a good run!

If your Lab has some physical limitations or if you have any doubts about his exercise needs, talk to your veterinarian. When you start an exercise program, start gradually, especially if your dog has been a couch potato. Sore muscles are no fun.

develop a type of hyperactivity when they eat a high calorie, high fat, high protein dog food. Other dogs have food allergies that might show up as behavior problems. If you have any questions about your dog's behavior in relation to food, or about the food you are feeding your dog, ask your veterinarian.

Play

Play is different from exercise, although exercise can be play. Laughter is very much a part of play and that is what makes it so special. Researchers know that laughter is wonderful medicine—it makes you feel better—and because of that, it has a special place in your relationship with your dog. If training is sometimes difficult, and your dog is getting into trouble, make time to play with him. Play is a great stress reliever; both for you and for your dog, so make some time every day to laugh and play.

Sometimes dogs will intentionally get into trouble because they feel ignored. To some dogs, negative attention (corrections, yelling and screaming) is better than no attention. By setting some time aside just for your Lab, you can avoid some of these situations.

HOUSEHOLD RULES

You may even need to institute some new household rules for you and other family members. Your dog can't raid the trash cans if you take the trash cans out before they are overflowing and put the trash cans away before you leave the house. Your Lab will get into less trouble if everyone would close closet doors, pick up dirty laundry and pick up their toys.

PREVENT PROBLEMS FROM HAPPENING

Because so many of the things we consider problems are not problems to your dog,

you need to prevent them from happening as much as possible when you are not there to teach him. If your Lab finds out how much fun it is to chew up your sofa cushion, throwing stuffing all over, you may have a difficult time stopping him. The same applies to the kitchen trash can that is full of scraps (treasures to your food motivated Lab!), the fruit trees in the backyard, and the children's toys. It's much easier to prevent a problem from happening than it is to break a bad habit.

Preventing a problem from happening might require you to fence off the garden, build some new, higher shelves in the garage or maybe even build your Lab a new dog run.

Part of preventing problems from happening also requires that you limit your dog's freedom. A young puppy or an untrained dog should never have unsupervised free run of the house; there is just too much he can get into. Instead, keep him in the room with you either by watching him or better yet, using baby gates across the doorways. If you can't keep him with you, then put him in his crate or outside in his yard.

BUILD YOUR LAB A DOG RUN

Make the run big enough so that he can move around and trot back and forth. Make sure there is shade, unspillable water and shelter from bad weather. When you leave him in the run, give him a toy or a treat and leave a radio on a soft, easy listening station in a nearby window.

DEALING WITH SPECIFIC PROBLEMS

Digging and Destroying the Garden

If your backyard looks like a military artillery range, you need to concentrate first on preventing these things from happening when you are not there to supervise your dog. If you come home eight to ten hours later and try to correct your dog for the hole he dug when you left for work, you are wasting your time; your correction is much too late. Instead of understanding that he is being corrected for digging, your Lab is going to think he's being corrected for you coming home.

When you're home, let your dog out for supervised runs in the backyard. When he starts to get into trouble, you can

interrupt his actions and teach him what is acceptable and what is not.

The destructive dog also needs exercise, training and play times every day to use up energy, stimulate his mind and spend time with you.

Most importantly, don't let your Labrador landscape artist watch you garden; if you do, he will come to you later with all of those bulbs you planted earlier!

The Barker

Are your neighbors complaining because your Lab is serenading the neighborhood when you're at work? Labs are not typically problem barkers but they will bark if bored and lonely.

Start by teaching him to be quiet while you're at home. When your dog starts barking, tell him "Quiet!" When he stops barking, praise him, "Good boy to be quiet!"

When he understands what you want, go for a short walk outside, leaving your dog at home. Listen and when you hear him start barking, come back and correct him. After a few corrections, when your dog seems to have the idea, ask your neighbor to help you. Go outside, out front, and have your neighbor come out and talk. Maybe the kids can play and create a distraction. When your dog barks, run back home as fast as you can and correct him again. Repeat as often as you need until he understands.

EXTRA HELP

Problem barkers may need extra help. There are anti-bark collars on the market, and several are humane and effective. All are triggered by the dog's barking and administer a correction to the dog. Some collars make a high-pitched sound, one squirts a whiff of citronella and others administer an electric shock. I do not recommend the shock treatment for most dogs; many will panic when corrected this way. However, the first two collars are quite effective with many dogs.

Some dogs will stop barking as you leave if you make leaving home very low-key and unexciting. A distraction also works well for many dogs. Take a small brown paper lunch bag and put a couple of treats in it. Maybe a dog biscuit, a piece of carrot, a slice of apple and a small toy. Tape the top shut and rip a very tiny hole in the side of the bag. As you walk out the door or the gate, give this

to your Lab. He will be so busy trying to figure out what's inside that he won't pay attention to you leaving.

Dashing Through Doors and Gates

This is actually one of the easiest problems to correct. Teach your Lab to sit and stay at all doors and gates and to hold that stay until you either give him permission to go through or release him after you have closed the door. By teaching him that doors and gates are boundaries that require permission, you will eliminate the problem.

Start with your dog on a leash and walk him up to the door. Have him sit, tell him to stay, and then with the leash firmly grasped in your hand, open the door wide and stand aside. If he dashes forward, correct him for breaking his stay, "No, stay!" Take him back where he started and do it again. If he continues to do it, give him a snap and release of the leash and collar as you correct him verbally. When he will hold the stay at this door, go to other doors and gates and teach the same lesson, the same way.

If your Lab tries to sneak past you when he is not on

the leash, block him with your leg or slam the door in his face as you give him a verbal correction.

If your dog does make it outside, don't chase him. If you chase him it becomes a game. Use your shaker to call him to you, "Sweetie, do you want a cookie? Come! Good boy!" When you do catch him or he comes back to you, don't correct him. If you do, he learns that coming back to you results in a correction. Instead, praise him for coming to you.

Jumping on People

Labs are solid, muscular dogs and can cause great damage if they jump on people. Your Lab can't jump on you or other people if he's sitting; it's physically impossible to do both of those things at the same time. Since your dog jumps on people for attention, if you teach him to sit when you pet you can eliminate the jumping.

When you come home from work and your dog is excited to see you, don't try to greet him with your arms full. Instead, greet him with empty hands. Then, when he tries to jump, grab him by the collar or the scruff of the neck and tell him to sit. When he sits, praise him, "Good boy to sit!" and pet him. If he tries to jump up again, use your hands to put him back into the sitting position.

If your Lab is really excited and it's very hard for him to control himself, once he's sitting, roll him over onto his back and give him a belly rub and a massage. This is still giving him the attention he needs but it is relaxing him at the same time.

OTHER PROBLEMS?

Many behavior problems can be solved, or at least controlled, by using similar techniques. Try to figure out why your Lab is doing what he's doing (from his point of view, not yours), what you can do to prevent the problem from happening and what you can do to use your training skills to teach your dog. Remember that a correction alone will not solve the problem; you need to prevent the problem as much as possible and also teach your dog what he can do.

If you still have some unresolved problems or if your dog is showing aggressive tendencies, then contact your local dog trainer or behaviorist for expert help.

Make sure your Lab gets plenty of exercise, playtime, and attention from you. Problem behavior often is the result of a bored or underexercised dog.

You can also use the leash to teach your Lab not to jump. When you are out for a walk and see your neighbor, don't let your neighbor pet your Lab until you make him sit. If he starts to jump on your neighbor, use a snap and release of the leash and a verbal correction, "No jump! Sit." Use the same technique when guests come to your house; leash your dog before they come in.

The key to correcting jumping on people is to make sure that the bad behavior is not rewarded. If someone pets your dog when he jumps up, the bad behavior is rewarded. When he learns that he gets all of the attention when he's sitting, then he will start sitting automatically for petting and when he does, praise him enthusiastically!

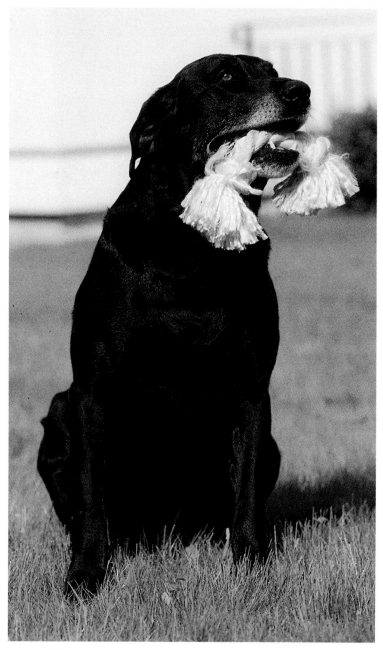

Your Labrador Retriever will enjoy hours of fun with a Nylafloss® , a tug toy made of nylon that literally flosses your dog's teeth while he plays.

Have Some
FUN
With Your Training!

HAVE FUN

Training has a tendency to be serious; after all, much of training is teaching your Labrador what his place in the family is and how to control himself. That can be serious stuff. However, training can also be fun. Games and trick training can challenge your training skills and your Lab's ability to learn. However, once you have taught your dog, you can have a great time showing off your dog's tricks, amusing your friends and family and just plain having fun with your dog.

RETRIEVING

Most Labrador Retrievers are, as the name suggests, born retrievers, willing and able to bring back anything that moves or is thrown. However, some will chase after whatever is thrown but don't always bring it back. If your Lab likes to retrieve then all you need to do is fine tune the game so that he brings the item all the way back to you and gives it to you without playing tug of war. If he hesitates on the way back, simply call him to you. If he drops the item, send him

Retrieving allows your Lab to use his natural instincts.

labrador retriever

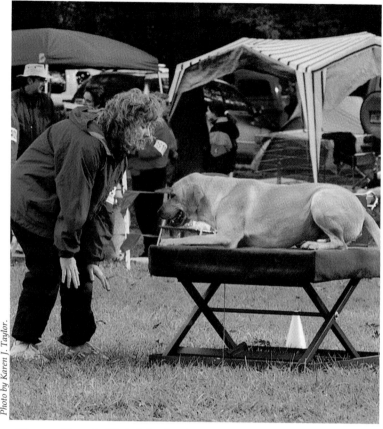

Photo by Karen J. Taylor.

The versatile and athletic Labrador Retriever can be trained to excel in many events, including agility.

back to it, again using encouragement to have him pick it up and bring it to you. Don't scold him or try to correct him; that will only serve to discourage him.

If your dog likes to take the thrown item and run with it, playing keep away, you have two options. You can stop the game and go inside, leaving him alone. This shows him that you will not chase him and the game will end when he tries to play keep away. Or you can have a long leash (a length of clothesline rope) on him when you start the game so that if he tries to play keep away, you can step on the rope, stop him, and use the rope to bring him back to you. If you need to use the rope, you still must praise him for

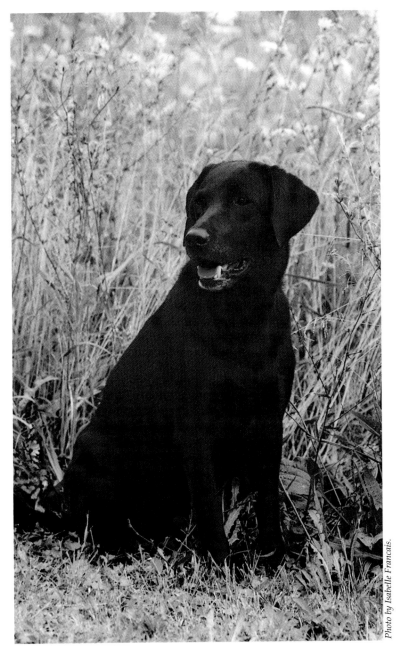

Photo by Isabelle Francais.

Have fun with your Labrador Retriever! His love of the outdoors will make your dog happy to participate in any activity.

labrador retriever

There are all kinds of flying disks for dogs and kids, but only one brand is made just for dogs with strength, scent, and originality. The Nylabone® Frisbee™ is a must if you want to have fun with your Lab.

coming back to you even if you made him do it. As has been said previously, the come comand must be positive.

Once your Lab is retrieving reliably and bringing the toy back to you, there are unlimited games you can play. Most Labrador Retrievers are born with a tennis ball in their mouth, so that is the obvious game of choice for many. To make it challenging, tennis balls can be throw short or far, or bounced off the side of the house. If your Lab is really dedicated, throw several tennis balls and see how many he can pick up and carry at once!

ONLY USE TOYS MADE FOR DOGS

Nylabone® Frisbees™ made especially for dogs are great fun. Throw the Frisbee™ and encourage your dog to chase it. When he jumps up after it, praise him enthusiastically. Go to a toy store and look in the aisle where Frisbees™ and balls are displayed. There are a variety of toys there that can make good retrieving dog toys; just keep your dog's safety in mind.

THE NAME GAME

The name game is a great way to make your dog think. And don't doubt him for a minute, your dog can think and is capable of learning the names of many different items and people. Not only is this a great game for your Lab, but it can come in handy around the house. Tell your dog to find your keys, or your shoes. Send your Lab after the remote control to the television, or to go find mom or dad. Plus, it's great fun to show off to your friends or guests!

Start with two items that are very different, perhaps a tennis ball and a bowl. Sit on the floor with your Lab and those two items, and have some treats that he likes. Tell him, "Where's the ball?" and bounce the ball so that he tries to grab it or at least, pays attention to it. When he touches it, tell him, "Good boy to find the ball!" and give him a treat.

When he is responding to the ball, then lay it on the floor next to the bowl and send him after it. Praise and reward him for getting it. Now set several different items out with the bowl and ball, and send him again. When he brings back the ball, praise and reward him. When he is doing that well,

place one of his toys out there, too, and send him. If he goes for his other toy, take it away, with no comment, and send him after the ball again. This is a critical step in his learning process and you may need to repeat it several times.

When he will pick up his ball from among several different items, including other toys, then start hiding the ball. Make it simple to start, maybe just partially hidden under a magazine. As he gets better, start making it more challenging.

When you can hide the tennis ball and your dog can find it, start teaching him the names of other items, following the same process. You will find that the first three items will be the most difficult. Your dog needs to learn how to learn and he needs to understand the concept you are trying to teach him. Once he understands that each of these things has a different sound, and that he needs to listen to you say those sounds, then he will start learning much faster.

HIDE AND SEEK

Hide and seek is a fun game, much like the hide and seek you played as a child, except that you (or other family members) will hide and your Lab will find you. Your dog will be much better at finding than you ever were, though, because he has such a sensitive nose and outstanding scenting abilities.

Start by teaching a family member's name (or your own) using the techniques you learned in the name game. When your dog can identify a family member, you can use

daughter!" and let him go. If he starts to look around and sniff, just be quiet and let him work and think. If your dog starts to look flustered or confused, tell him again, "Go find daughter!" and help him find her. When he goes to daughter, praise him enthusiastically and let daughter give your dog the treat.

As your dog gets better at this game, you can start making it

Puppies love to play games, especially things like hide and seek. Play training can help your puppy develop cognitive skills and master the learning process.

that family member to hide. Give that family member a treat and have her show your dog that she has one. Hold your Lab as that family member goes and hides in a fairly easy location. Tell your dog, "Go find

more challenging. Have family members hide in more difficult places or slightly farther away from your Lab. They can also run around a little before finding a hiding place, so that there is a more challenging trail. As your

Lab gets better, you can also cover his eyes so that he can't see the family member go hide.

When your dog has learned the names of different family members and knows how to find them, you can use this skill around the house. Send your Lab out to the yard to get the kids when it's dinner time. Or have him take the remote control to dad when he asks for it. Hide and seek is a lot of fun, is challenging for your dog and uses his natural scenting abilities.

THE COME GAME
In this game, two family members will stand or sit across the room or yard from each other. Each will have some treats for your Lab. Taking turns, each will call your dog to come and when he does, praise and reward him. This is a very simple game but gives you a chance to practice the come command and makes it fun at the same time. Plus, everyone in the family can practice it, giving even the kids a chance to "train" your dog.

A Lab retrieves sticks thrown into the ocean.

SHAKE HANDS

Shaking hands is a very easy trick to teach your dog. Have your Lab sit in front of you and ask him to "Shake" as you reach behind one front paw and tickle his leg in the hollow just behind his paw. When he lifts his paw to escape the tickle, shake his paw as you tell him, "Good to shake!" and give him a treat. When he starts to lift his paw on his own, stop tickling.

labrador retriever

WAVE

When he is shaking hands reliably, tell him "Shake. Wave!" and instead of shaking his paw, just lightly touch your hand under his paw and move your hand away so that he continues to reach for your hand. As he reaches for your hand, tell him, "Good to wave!" With the wave, you want him to lift his paw higher than in the shake and to move it up and down so that he looks like he is waving.

TREAT ON NOSE

Have your Lab sit and stay. Hold his chin with one hand as you place a treat on the top of his nose. Tell him "Stay!" After a few seconds, tell him, "Okay!" and let him toss the treat and catch it. Gradually increase the time you want him to wait before you release him and enthusiastically praise him when he catches the treat in midair.

ROLL OVER

Have your Lab lie down. With a treat in one hand, circle your Lab's head with the treat in the direction you want him to roll, while you tell him, "Roll over!" At first, you may need to physically help him roll. Praise him when he does roll over, even if you need to help him. Enthusiastically praise him when he does it on his own.

Treat on nose.

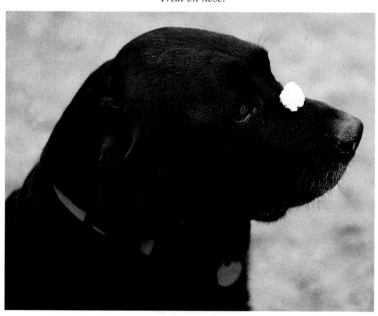

Once he can roll over by himself, you can ask him to do it more than once. Have him roll over two or three times. Teach him a command for each, "Three roll overs!" or "Two roll overs!" Impress your friends that your dog knows how to count!

Steps in rolling-over training

AND THERE'S MORE!
Trick training is limited only to what you want to teach your dog. Teach him to crawl, to play dead or to sit up and beg. Teach him to dance. What would you (and your dog!) enjoy?

Good Dog!

l a b r a d o r   r e t r i e v e r

SUGGESTED
READING

BOOKS BY T.F.H. PUBLICATIONS

JG-109
Training The Perfect Puppy
By Andrew DePrisco
160 pages, over 200 color photos

TS-205
Successful Dog Training
By Michael Kamer, OSB
160 pages, over 150 color photos

TS-258
Training Your Dog for Sports and
Other Activities
By Charlotte Schwartz
160 pages, 170 full-color photos

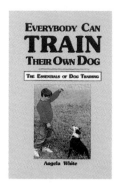

TW-113
Everybody Can Train
Their Own Dog
By Angela White
256 pages, 200 color photos

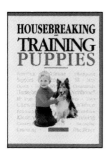

WW-009
Housebreaking and Training Puppies
By J.R. Gardner
64 pages, 79 full-color photos

WW-025
Dog Obedience Training
By Ross Allan
64 pages, over 100 full-color photos

TS-252
Dog Behavior and Training
By Lowell Ackerman, DVM
288 pages, over 170 full-color photos

KW-022
Basic Dog Training
By Miller Watson
96 pages, over 100 full-color photos

JG-117
Dog Training
By Dorman Pantfoeder
160 pages, over 100 full-color photos

TS-283
Training Problem Dogs
By Dr. Louis Vine
256 pages, 50 drawings

JG-107
*A New Owner's Guide to
Labrador Retrievers
By Mary Feazell
160 pages, 150 full-color photos*

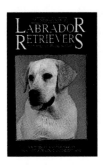

BB-113
*Dr. Ackerman's Book of
Labrador Retrievers
Lowell Ackerman, DVM
96 pages, 75 full-color photos*

KW-40S
*Labrador Retrievers
Diane McCarty
224 pages, 195 full-color photos*

RE-302
*Guide to Owning a Labrador Retriever
Richard T. Burrows
64 pages, 50 color photos*

TS-241
*Official Book of the
Labrador Retriever
The Labrador Retriever Club
416 pages, full-color throughout*

PS-805
*The Labrador Retriever
Dorothy Howe and
Anna Katherine Nicholas
352 pages, 190 full-color photos*